MW01712788

# Christian Bikers Across America

Angel Kensler

Fairway Press
Lima, Ohio

CHRISTIAN BIKERS ACROSS AMERICA

FIRST EDITION


Library of Congress Catalog Card Number: 96-84072

ISBN 0-7880-0674-6

PRINTED IN U.S.A.

## *DEDICATION*

*This book is dedicated to all Bikers who left the ways of the world to follow Jesus. May you always press on so that we will see each other in Heaven. Matthew 4:19: "And he saith unto them follow me, and I will make you fishers of men." Ephesians 5:1-2: "Be ye therefore followers of God, as dear children: And walk in love, as Christ also hath loved us, and hath given himself for us an offering and a sacrifice to God for a sweet smelling aroma." A special thanks to the people who helped me get this done. Also to my son Rick and daughter Casey that I love them enough not to leave for good.*

*Cover by John Burke, and special thanks to "Buzz."*

# Table of Contents

# Foreword

Let's take a look at the average hardcore Biker in general, all around the world.

It usually starts out looking for brotherhood or someone with whom you have the same interest, riding with the wind in your face, just being free, knowing by twisting the throttle you control the power of the big V twin with the thunder sound in the background . . . just man and machine. Before long you start hanging out at your favorite pub, then a few more bro's and a few more ladies and just a little more drugs, just being yourself not even realizing the web has been set. Just taking care of club business. I used to think the party and hurting people and everything that went with it was just our kind of lifestyle; but to most, it became our nightmare! Sooner or later it became a territorial thing. If you've never been there, it's hard to try to explain the loyalty of most clubs. As you go through these pages, try to go a little deeper to come to know what kind of people they were and what kind of people they are now. If you look real close in this paragraph you will get a look at the whole picture.

Yo, Jesus, it's me, a down and out scooter tramp. I know I don't need to tell you who I am 'cause you already know all about me. But even though I have a lot of people around me and guns and money and a lot of fine women and I've shared in a lot of pleasurable sin, I hurt a lot of people in the name of business. But today, there's no one around. I hate the man I became. Today I started on the road alone, tomorrow I may face death row with many people watching, but in reality, I'm still alone. It wasn't supposed to go this far. It just got out of hand, trying harder and harder to prove myself. When ego set in, so did pride. No one made me choose that road but myself. But the adventure, the black leather jacket, the power of the motor, being free in the wind and the idea of other people being afraid of you, just added to the excitement. You see, even though you knew who I was, I didn't know anything about you. And what I did know, I didn't think you would want someone with long hair and tattoos all over . . . all the things I did . . . I thought I went over the edge!!! For how could you forgive someone like that?

I know now, it was your love and grace, that you died for Bikers too . . . THANKS!

# Introduction

# Christian Bikers Across America

There are a lot of secular things out there about Bikers but not too many about Christian Bikers. This is a guide so that you can go from coast to coast with testimony of sold out brothers and a few sisters for Jesus and their ministries.

You'll meet Brothers who could never sit in the same room together because of a patch on their backs. But now they not only sit in the room with each other but they talk, laugh, hug, and pray together, despite their different patches. The bottom line is seeing people's lives turned around for Jesus.

When a Christian Biker sees a brother or sister turn their lives over to Jesus most of us know where they've been. You all know the saying, "Been there, done that!"

By reading these testimonies I hope you come to know these brothers and sisters, but most of all *I hope you will come to know Jesus as your Lord and Savior.*

# A Rebel With A Cause

# Bikers For Christ With Pastor Fred Z

I may not look like your ordinary Christian. I have long hair, a beard, an earring, and I wear a black leather jacket with a club patch on the back. I'm a member of Bikers for Christ, a Christian Biker organization. I visit places that few people would dare go. I scan heavy metal concert crowds looking for young people with a deadly attraction for the fast lane. I hang out with Bikers, drug addicts, hookers, and wayward teenagers. The street people know me simply as Fred Z. When I find them, I tell them about Jesus and they listen.

From the time I was thirteen years old until I met the Lord, I used and sold drugs. Later in life, I rode choppers and chose the life that I wanted to live. Not many things slowed me down, not a drug bust in the 70s, a stint in the military, not even drug overdoses. However, one thing did slow me down. In 1974, I crashed a motorcycle into a stone wall.

I'll never forget that crash. A friend and I were cruising down an unfamiliar road at about 85 miles an hour when a sharp corner loomed ahead. Realizing I couldn't make the turn, I looked for a way out. To my left was a small dirt road. Dense foliage obscured my vision of what was down the road, but I decided it was my only chance. As I turned down the road, I looked up and saw a stone wall about twenty feet ahead.

Panicking, I down-shifted and braked as fast as I could, hitting the front brake lever so hard that the metal lever broke off in my hand. I could feel my heart racing uncontrollably as I anticipated the worst. We were still doing about fifty mph when the bike slammed into the wall. On impact, my friend (who was on the back) flew over me and the wall. He rolled a few times, then got up with only a few minor cuts and some sore ribs. As my body lunged forward, I heard a loud crack. My face bounced off the gas tank and handlebars, and my left leg was jammed under a lip at the bottom of the gas tank. The impact ripped a hole in my leg four inches around and two inches deep, missing the main artery by a hair. By the time the paramedics arrived, I was delirious with shock, screaming about my bike, kicking and clawing at them as they lowered me onto a stretcher. They had to hit me up with Demerol three times before I calmed down.

Hours later, I woke up in the hospital at Milford, Massachusetts. My back was broken, and I was bleeding from the spine.

This became a turning point in my life. For the next eight months while recovering from my injuries, I began thinking about God, and what life was all about. Often I thought back over my young years, and the life I had lived . . .

For me, rebellion had been a way of life. At age thirteen, I started smoking grass and drinking beer. When I didn't have enough money for a sixpack or a bag of weed, I'd get together with my buddies and we would sniff glue or gasoline.

At fourteen, I graduated to speed, downers, and sex. Soon I was into LSD two or three times a week. I even took it while in classes at school. At sixteen, I had my first experience with Bikers. I was at a parade when about fifteen outlaws pulled up and began to party. They defied anyone who challenged them. Soon two Bikers from a rival club rode up, and a fight broke out. One guy was cutting at another's ear with a beer can pull tab. It was radical! I was actually rooting for them . . . like a Roman cheering the gladiators.

Soon afterward, I started working at a Harley Davidson motorcycle shop in Boston, cleaning and waxing the new bikes — and dreaming of the day that I would be a Biker, too. I saved up a few bucks and bought an old 65cc Harley. Although it was small, I had a great time riding it in the fields and dirt roads near my home. At seventeen, my dependence on drugs grew stronger. I started eating reds and ludes like they were candy. I also tried snorting and shooting heroin. To support my habit, I had to rip off cars and break into houses for money.

Eventually, I dropped out of school, and began hitch-hiking across the country, ending up at a large anti-war demonstration in Washington, D.C. Everyone that was anyone in the anti-war movement was there — the Yippies, Black Panthers, the Weathermen. Everyone was loaded on drugs and planning to take over Washington for a day. We figured that it would show the government our strength; then they'd listen to our cause. I really believed in what the radicals were attempting, so I joined the Yippie movement.

There was a concert at the beginning of the demonstration. At the concert I found a guy that was selling LSD, and I bought a four-way hit of Orange sun-shine. Counting on my high tolerance for drugs, I took the whole thing. For hours after the hit, it seemed like the Washington Monument was melting right before my eyes like a huge candle. Finally, I was taken to a medical tent screaming. But when the acid wore off, I rejoined the action. By this time, the radicals were getting violent. At one point, I saw National Guardsmen moving toward us, shooting tear gas into the crowd. People were screaming and running everywhere.

I was among the many who were arrested and herded like cattle into a large stadium (the jails were already full). Toward the end of the day, the authorities were letting us go, if we promised to leave D.C. and never return.

My radical lifestyle soon landed me in jail. The law gave me a choice — go to prison or join the military. I arrived at Great Lakes Naval Training Center less than two weeks later. Even the military became a joke to me. Within a few months, I was back to dealing drugs again and getting into more trouble.

I was trained as a ground support technician. One night while on duty, a friend and I smoked some really strong dope. I became so stoned that I ran the tail section of a jet fighter into the guard rails at the fuel pit. The damage was estimated at $200,000. I blamed the accident on poor lighting and was let off the hook.

While in the Navy, I bought my first large street bike, an 850cc Norton Commando. I raced people for cases of beer and bags of dope, and rode with a bike club. It was during this time that I had my accident.

Finally, I was discharged from the Navy. I went home for a few months but couldn't handle being tied down. Even with a large metal brace strapped to my back, I left home again, eventually heading up to Alaska. I fit right in with the locals and was soon back to partying. I got myself another bike and hung out at the favorite beer joints.

From the time of my accident, I had been doing a lot of soul-searching. Eastern religions were of particular interest to me. Often I sat around reading the Bhagavad Gita and other Eastern literature and meditating.

One day a Christian girl invited me to her church. I smoked a few joints and figured I'd just go in there and tell those Christian how deceived they were. But I didn't count on the power of the Holy Spirit.

The preacher of that charismatic church seemed to be talking directly to me. Slowly my defenses broke down. I could feel something tugging inside me. So when the altar call was given, I ran down the aisle. I accepted the Lord, was baptized in water, and filled with the Spirit all in the same night.

My life changed radically. God had given me the gift of evangelism. The next few months, the church people watched in wonder as this long-haired guy with Harley wings on his jacket herded his vanload of young people into the church every week. I served the Lord at that church for a year, and even tried going to Bible school.

But something was wrong. Although I was filled with a lot of zeal and emotion, I wasn't grounded in the Lord. Before I knew it, my "old nature" started rearing its ugly head. My Christian experience seemed like a yo-yo. For a few months, I'd do great, then go back to partying (weakened), then make a comeback to the Lord.

During this time, I met a beautiful girl named Sydney. We began dating, fell in love, and married a few months later. At first, things went well for us. However, worldly desires crept back in, and we slipped away into our former way of life.

We left Alaska and finally settled in northern California. The change in scenery didn't help. Because of the instability of my spiritual leadership and lack of priorities, our marriage collapsed.

During the hard times that followed, I really got serious with the Lord and accepted His rule in my life. Shortly after I began divorce proceedings, Syd contacted me. She was living in a Christian community called Jesus People U.S.A. in Chicago, and had also given the Lord full reign in her life. I stopped the divorce proceedings, moved out to Chicago, and we allowed God to totally heal our broken marriage. Within a few months, we were back together again. That was four years ago.

The Lord called us into ministry, and we have found our church home at Calvary Chapel. Since we both have made Jesus our Lord, He has blessed our family beyond measure. We now have three beautiful little girls — Melody, Sandra, and Andrea. With our histories of drug and alcohol abuse, we thank God for His mercy in giving us three perfectly healthy little girls.

I am now an ordained minister of Calvary Chapel. God has given me a burden to reach out to Bikers, drug addicts, cultists, and teenagers. I've helped start three Christian motorcycle ministries. I'm a member of the I.C.B.A. (International Christian Bikers Association).

I love all people and try to share the love of Jesus with all that I meet. He has done many miracles in my life.

We use our motorcycles as tools for evangelism, sharing the gospel on the streets with everyone we meet. I've had the pleasure of bringing the gospel into jails, juvenile halls, and hospitals. I've also been active in promoting Christian rock bands that offer an alternative for young people. We've seen many backsliders reconciled and many souls saved in the last few years.

Jesus has freed me from the bondage of drugs, alcohol and sin. I've discovered that serving Jesus is the only way to have peace and real purpose for my life.

"Some wish to live within the sound of church or chapel bells, we want to run a rescue shop within a yard of hell."

You can write or call for more information:

Pastor Fred Z.    Bikers For Christ
c/o Calvary Chapel
P.O Box 1106
Marysville, CA  95901
Phone (916) 743-6720

# Personal Testimony Of Gailen "Mac" Stone

My name is Gailen Stone. Most people call me "Mac." I was born in Minneapolis, Minnesota, to good Scandinavian parents in 1951. My mom was a homemaker and stayed home to raise us kids until I was in Junior High School; then during that time she took a job outside the home. My dad was an over-the-road truck driver which caused him to be gone a lot. But according to him, "What else is a former dairy farmer, without a high school education, going to do to raise and feed eight kids?" My parents were good parents, as I stated. They taught us good moral values. They brought us to church every Sunday and Wednesday. Many of my friends thought that my dad was a preacher because we went to church so much and he was so "straight." No drinking, smoking, and so forth.

Many people claim that the reason for their bad behavior is the fault of their parents, or society. I honestly do not believe that my folks, or society, are to blame in any way for how I was going to choose to live for the first decade of my adult life.

At fifteen I just up and left school one day and decided to go to California. I didn't have any money, nor did I even really know how to get to California. I did know that if I stayed on U.S. Highway 10 (which went right through our town of Anoka, Minnesota) I would get to Seattle, Washington. From there I would figure out how to get to San Francisco. As it turned out I was only on the west coast for about three weeks before realizing that I wanted to go home. Probably the most significant thing that happened was that I learned to smoke "pot" and really acquired a taste for it.

I turned sixteen shortly after my trip to California. It was at this time that I really started to use a lot of drugs and alcohol. I would lie to my parents as to where I would be or just outright rebel against them. I became quite the fighter and had over 100 street fights before I graduated from school. Like the old country western song said, " . . . he's a nice guy when he's sober, but he stays drunk all the time. . . ." It was in those years that I noticed a group of motorcycle riders that rode Harley Davidson motorcycles, hung around in front of a small grocery store and drank beer. These guys seemed really "cool" to me and they sure rode "cool bikes." I had ridden small "bikes" since I was twelve. My dad had a 1945 H-D when he met my mom so we all were raised to believe that Harleys were the only way to go.

I started hangin' around when I was seventeen. I'd heard that these guys were 1% ers and that they were a bad bunch to be around. But they always treated me right. One day I just walked into the store and bought a quart of beer without the owner carding me. Outside I commented on this strange occurrence when one of the guys said, "It's 'cuz you're with us."

Shortly after this I purchased a 1955 K-model Harley. Even though it never ran all that good for me, just owning it made me more accepted by the "club guys." I was a quick understudy! I learned the ways of the Biker well. Things seemed to be going along quite smoothly in fact until I received my draft notice from the U.S. Army. I entered the Army in February of '71. Things went well at first but I attribute that mostly to lack of access to drugs or alcohol in basic training. After basic I slipped right back into the same screwed-up lifestyle. I went A.W.O.L. a couple of times and was eventually discharged for the "good of the service." It didn't take long for me to get right back into the bike scene. Most of those years are kind of a blur. Drinking, drugs, fighting, chasing women, day in, day out. I had a few brushes with the law for motorcycle theft and once for stabbing a guy in a bar (that's where I picked up the name "Mac The Knife"). I managed to get out of doing any hard-time through lawyers and probation.

I met my wife, Linette, in a bar in south Minneapolis in the winter of '75. She liked to party and liked Bikers so we hit it off pretty good. We decided to get married in the spring of 1976. The first date was postponed because she was unsure about me being able to support her so she left and went back to her ex-old man in Rhode Island. But because I hadn't cut her loose I went out and got her back. This didn't make her real happy, so even though she was back in Minnesota, we didn't see each other very much. Then one day in May on impulse we decided to get married. I suppose that under the circumstances our marriage was okay, but the "club" and partying always came first. So disaster was inevitable. I came home drunk one night and we got into one of our many arguments. I said something like this: "You don't love me . . . you won't even give me babies!" Well, that's one thing she could do. So, without telling me, she went off birth-control. You guessed it. She announced one day that she was pregnant. Even though she was pregnant she kept on working and supporting us because I was too involved in the club and partying. One day she'd had enough and told me that she had found a place to live and that she was leaving. We had been fighting so much that this was okay by me. I had the "prospects" come and help move her and I moved into the club house.

This all took place in the spring and summer of 1979. This was also the year when God really started to take action in my life. I went on a "run" in the end of April and failed to come home afterward. I went from Sioux City to Des Moines, Iowa, to party with some of the brothers there. While in Des Moines we borrowed a speed boat and a pontoon boat from a couple of "retired brothers" and went partying at a local lake. I was driving the pontoon boat with all of the "acid-heads" on board. The "downer-freaks" had the speed boat. As I recall it was dusk and because none of the boats had running lights we needed to get back to shore. The guys in the speed boat pulled up along side saying that they couldn't find the party spot. So we directed them assuming that they'd head back. They didn't. Instead they intended to buzz us one more time. When I finally spotted them the two guys in the speed boat were fighting over the steering wheel. As I looked over my shoulder I could see that they were going to hit us. The speed boat's bow came directly through our motor, breaking it in half. The bow then hit me between the shoulders and came to rest on my legs, pinning me and the lawn chair that I was sitting in under the speed boat, nearly capsizing the pontoon. One of the guys on my boat pushed the speed boat off. However, by then, I was starting to lose my breath and began sinking with the lawn chair wrapped around my legs. The water was dark and murky. It was then that I heard a voice. It said: "BREATHE IN, IT'S EASY TO DIE, BREATHE IN, IT'S EASY TO DIE." (It wasn't until more than a year later that I realized that Satan was trying to take my life.) The sun had set by now and it was really quite black under water. I was losing buoyancy and couldn't tell which way was up. Then suddenly I saw it. A shaft of bright yellow light. I knew that it had to be the way up to safety. As suddenly as I had seen the shaft of light, the chair that was so tightly entwined with my legs now fell free. I shot to the top like a Nautilus missile from a submarine. Breathing fresh air never felt so good. I had been quite high on "acid" and been drinking a lot but when I came out of the water I was stone-cold sober. I tried to get high and drunk all that night but to no avail. The next morning I was feeling quite depressed so I got on my chopper and road home to Minneapolis.

When I needed a clean, warm place to stay I would go to my wife's apartment but because I still wouldn't hold a job, or be responsible, she would only let me stay a day or two. Most of the summer of '79 was crazy. I crashed my Harley a couple of times. Fights were too numerous to count and I was even shot at a time or two. But as I look back God seemed to be sparing my life. In September of that year I took a job driving a semi-truck for one of my club brothers and my wife was getting close to having our first child, so we decided to give it another try and get a place together.

Our son Nick was born on October 31, which was one of the greatest days of my life. I HAD A SON! I still rode and partied with the club but began missing runs. The lifestyle was starting to lose its luster.

That fall was exceptionally warm so we rode well into November. One Friday night I was out riding with one of the prospects and got into a drag race with him. As we took off from the lights I throttled up and dropped the clutch. The bike literally exploded as the transmission broke in half and I coasted to a stop. The prospect, thinking he was really beating me bad, didn't stop until he got to the clubhouse. After a few minutes when I didn't follow, he came and "pegged me" back. I didn't let that stop me from partying though. I got my car and continued to drink until the bars closed. On the way home my car overheated and stalled so I just passed out behind the wheel alongside the road. I awoke some time later in the back seat of a squad car. When I came to I asked the cop how I got there. He said I walked. I said, "Hmmm." I then asked: "Did I give you a hard time?" He said, "No." I said, "Hmmm." This was not my normal behavior. I asked what was going to happen now. He said he was going to take me to detox. Knowing that he, by law, could not force me to detox, I asked what my options were. He said I could go to jail but that if we did that he would also write me up for DWI. (That meant a $375.00 fine, loss of license and a huge increase in insurance fees.) I opted for detox.

While in detox, I looked up and down the hall, seeing old chronic drunks to my left and young teenage rebels on my right. Those kids reminded me of myself in my younger days. I got to thinking, "If those kids on my right are what I was like, and this is me now, then what I have to look forward to (if I didn't die first) was becoming like those old chronics at the end of the hall." Somehow none of this seemed to appeal to me. After talking to a rehab counselor, who was an ex-member of another bike club, I agreed to go into a treatment center following the Thanksgiving holiday. The day when I was supposed to go to treatment I shocked myself. I decided to go! My wife helped me pack my duffel bag and as I was getting ready to leave I asked her where that old Bible was that my dad's church had given me for graduation from high school. She said, "It's right here," as she pulled it off the bookshelf and put it in my bag. I took the bus that day because she didn't drive. This was kind of a surprise because "Bikers don't do bus" but come to think of it "Bikers don't do treatment either." The coming days were full of many painful experiences.

I was to learn many things about myself that I really didn't want to hear. I learned through their counseling that I was an alcoholic and a drug addict. I was chemically dependent. I read lots of books and articles about addictions and human behavior in treatment, most of which was over my head. I read all the old National Geographics and about halfway through the thirty-day program found myself wanting things to read. One night I was having difficulty sleeping, couldn't find anything to read so I took out that Bible I'd brought along. I really didn't know where to start but remembered the Book of Revelation was supposed to be interesting. Kind of the "Rambo" stuff of the Bible. As I read Revelation I found it exciting with all the hail balls and wars of supernatural proportion; however, it was quite confusing, too. After finishing that book I decided that I would read the Gospel of John when I discovered that the same guy wrote both books. When I came to Chapter Three I recognized a verse from my youth: John 3:16 (NASB). "For God so loved the world, that He gave His only begotten Son, that whoever believes in Him should not perish, but have eternal life."

I also recall that there seemed to be an overwhelming sense of love as I read on. Well, in a short time I finished that book and was still unable to sleep so I looked for something else of interest. I then found the First Epistle.

I've since gone through Bible college and have been pastoring since 1984. I've been pastoring The Princeton Vineyard Christian Fellowship and I'm also the President of Bond-Slaves Christian M.C. which has given me the opportunity to go back into the same motorcycle community and witness for Jesus Christ. Jesus is Lord! To Him be the Glory.

For more information contact:

Mac Stone
Phone: (612) 389-4753

# Brother Bert
# A.K.A. The Gangster Of Love

Gonna make this short and sweet, depending on your taste. Mine, a common tale of drugs, women, smuggling, and so on, since I was fifteen. I mean two or three felonies by noon meant I'd overslept. Came from a home where I had love. My parents split up when I was eleven – boy, was I glad – some relationships shouldn't have been. Stuffed on a church bus young. Got the basics but no direction. Little was I to know I was being set-up, my whole life had been that way.

What's a young boy to do? At sixteen I got married. Hippie-gangster-smuggler-Biker, what was I anyway? Lost, that's for sure.

I went on in the stinking fast lane on the edge, trying to make a left turn. There was only one offramp and that was death. I didn't fear the valley of the shadow of death. I was the baddest dude in the valley, or so I thought. Boy, was I a fool.

After 47 felony arrests and no convictions, life was a joke. It's a who ya know world, and it still is . . . but it starts with Jesus . . . only know Jesus. That's when conviction came. Oh the power of the Lord – ya see, I was set up. This conviction was sweet and I love it. I saw my whole family saved, all my five brothers and my goody-two-shoes sister, too.

I went to hear my brother's testimony, stink . . . I thought we were going to eat, ya see . . . I was set up . . . like a bowling pin, like my many times before my arms went into the air . . . at age 29 I surrendered face down, palms up, nothing in my pockets. Oh, what a rush. My mind at a million miles a second as his blood washed me clean. What's a boy to do? Go to Baptist college . . . ya see . . . me clean shaven, three-piece suit . . . I felt like I was going to court every day . . . so what I wanted, more Jesus. Had to have more.

Then it came, had to leave the church; I was a little too crazy for them.

So we started our own, fourteen of us turned into 6,000 and, you got it, I was set-up. Assistant Pastor, Deacon, Counselor, many titles. But I knew the one that fit . . . sinner-servant-saint. That bunch turned into over thirty fellowship churches and many are still moving on . . . me, I got the boot again. I was a little too crazy so I wore T-shirts that said "Satan Sucks," "God Rules," "Hell with the Devil." Get the picture? Now you see, and as for me I wanted to go back to the patch-wearing Biker, back to the camps of old to share the good news of His love. The Christian bike club at that time threw me out. I knew again I was set-up.

What was I to do . . . start my own. That I did. I know it was Christ who did it all — wonderful things kept happening. Preached in Russia, Norway, Finland, Spain, all through U.S. and Mexico. Still I knew . . . I was set-up. Got married, didn't last, got divorced. My club kicked me out. Never felt so free in my life. Back on the road, highway and byways. Of course my ex-wife forgave me, as did my Lord and King. Others still have a problem . . . I don't, ain't going to clean it up. My Father did with the blood of His Son, for a rat like me. Oh, the power of Jesus. I was never worthy. But because of the cross I'm truly free in deed. Seven kids, six grandkids all know Jesus. They also know that I fall short. Like the Apostle Paul I know I'm the Chief of Sinners. But if our Lord can use a stinking donkey, He can and will use me. And you. Hate the sin but love the sinner. Let all know about his forgiveness. 'Cuz, if you ain't sick, you don't need the doctor. Others, doctors practice — Jesus heals. Wake up and die right, fool. Don't be spiritually constipated or a stinkin pew porker 'cuz our Lord wants righteous fruit not religious nuts. Get on with it no matter what happens. F.T.W. do ya know what that meant in early Biker world? "FOREVER TOGETHER WHATEVER," "TILL THE STINKIN' WHEELS FALL OFF." I know if I do what the Lord wants me to do, I won't have to do what he doesn't want me to do. As for me and my house we will serve the Lord through his forgiveness at the cross. Oh, the power of His

Blood. I got mine — I know that I know that I know.

Christ's Love,
Brother Bert

Isaiah 6:8
AKA The Gangster of Love, ya see what I mean? I was set up.
A Soldier, Set Free

# Charlie's Story

Before sharing my story with ya, I'd like to first tell you that I am not special or different than anyone else out there. My purpose in sharing my story is not to glorify the lifestyle I lived, but it is, in fact, meant to glorify God who saved me from myself by teaching me the simplistic task of dying to my flesh daily and living to meet the needs of others.

I can remember through the fifteen years of drunkenness someone always coming around me to tell me about Jesus. They would tell me to repeat this simple prayer and my life would be turned around. They always seemed to get me when life was at its lowest. I thought, "What do I have to lose?" so I said their prayer. After that I never saw them again, my life was still crap, so I went back to what was familiar to me: drinking and drugs. After enough times of trial and error I gave up on any hope in God. After all, if he is the one who controls everything, then he was the reason for my problems, not the solution! God got the blame for everything, and his faithful servants usually got the back of my hand for even mentioning him to me. My last few years as a drunk I was barely acceptable to even go outside. I lived like an animal and rarely even spoke to people. Most of the time I was like a screaming lunatic.

One night a few friends wanted to go out drinking in the local bars. It didn't take a whole lot of convincing on their part for me to go along. None of us had a driver's license or up-to-date registration or any real reason to be on the road. We were pretty well wasted before we went out. Larry was always out of a job and looking for work. Danny was an odd jobs type of guy, would do about anything for a buck. Well, the three of us hit the road with Larry driving. I rode shotgun, and Danny was in the back. After hammering another six-pack at the bar I decided to head on home and grab a couple twelve packs and settle down to some serious drinking. On the way home Larry and Danny started arguing and Danny started to punch Larry in the head. I turned around and shoved Danny back in his seat and told him to knock it off before he gets us in a wreck. All was quiet for about a minute and then Danny from behind me grabs me by the throat in a head lock and starts to pull me into the back seat by my neck while he was pounding on my face. It took a while but I finally broke his grip, and as I was about to deliver an attitude adjuster Danny opened the door and jumped out. He rolled up onto the sidewalk and we pulled into a liquor store about a hundred feet away. Larry went in to buy some more beer and I went back to finish what Danny had started.

I don't even know who threw the first punch but the fight was on! All of a sudden I felt a sharp pain in my shoulder. I backed away from him when I realized that he stabbed me. He charged me and stabbed me two more times and I hit the ground like a sack of potatoes. I remember seeing him running away. My stomach was cut all the way across and I had to hold it together as I staggered back to the liquor store to get Larry. I walked into the store looking for Larry and he was standing in line with a twelve pack. I told Larry I was stabbed and we needed to go to the hospital. Larry decided to wait and pay for his twelve pack first. Pretty soon I had a large crowd standing there staring at me and as I looked down there was already a large puddle of blood that was pouring out of me. We finally made it back to the car and would have made it to the hospital in about three minutes except Larry was pretty well drunk and got lost trying to find it. By now I was going in and out from losing so much blood. I saw the light by the hospital and told Larry to head towards the light. Larry pulled up in front of the hospital where an ambulance driver grabbed him and told him you can't park here. Larry starts arguing with him saying, "But I didn't stab him." As these two start going at it in the parking lot I decided my only chance was to make it to the doors. I crawled to the doors and passed out just shy of the entrance. I had lost so much blood that my wife was picked up and told that I was not expected to live.

Within the next hour my heart stopped twice. After getting me stable I went in for emergency surgery. After three days in critical care I woke up. I had over two thousand stitches holding me together with tubes and drains coming out all over me. My first question to the doctor was why did you bother? Instead of the lecture I expected he asked the nurse to leave and he pulled the curtain around and sat at the foot of my bed. He told me that I am a searcher, and that I've been trying to find where I belong. I looked in drugs and alcohol for years trying to fit in. He said that there is only one who can fill that void in my life and that was Jesus. I listened politely, after all the guy just saved my life. After that for the next five days I have never seen as many Christians that just started coming to my room. My nurse was a Christian, the officer in charge of my case was a Christian, everyone I came into contact with was a Christian.

After I got out of the hospital Sunday came around and I was laying in bed watching television. The police officer in charge of my case came by. He said that there was a church in town that he goes to that had a lot of people just like me and asked if I wanted to check it out. So my first Sunday in church I came pulling up to church not knowing what to expect. It was a good service but I still did not feel a part of it.

They had a Drug and Alcohol Ministry at the church called Overcomers Outreach on Monday night. The pastor was one of the members. At this point is when I hit bottom. I had been out of the hospital for a while and I was wanting a drink real bad. Before going to that meeting I wanted to die because life was just too hard without alcohol. The feeling of discontentment was so strong that after the meeting I went back to church to tell someone what was really going on with me. The pastor sat and listened to me for a while and asked me if I knew Christ personally. I told him about my prayers before and how they were never answered. He told me to pray with him and to come to his office the next day where he would show me how to read the Bible. After that there was no getting rid of me. The church had become my safe place and a day didn't go past, without me being there. After six months I was called into the Pastor's office. They said that they had been praying about a new leader in the Overcomers group and asked about me doing it. I told them thanks but no thanks, I'm still wrestling with my own problems. The pastor would not let me turn it down and offered to help me in any way that he could.

That was seven years ago and I'm glad my pastor didn't give up on me as easy as I gave up on myself. I have since gone back to college and am presently a California State drug and alcohol counselor and I'm working on getting my masters degree in behavioral science. In my free time I'm usually found twisting the throttle of my faithful 75 shovelhead and riding with my bro's from Bikers For Christ.

Please send any inquiries to:

Charles Lincoln
1400 Segsworth Way #8
GrassValley, CA 95945

# The Christian Rider

You don't know me but I am your brother . . . and I am taking Him (Jesus), to the streets.

I know you have heard of Him ... King of Kings . . . Son of God . . . Savior of mankind. Jesus the Christ. He was sent by God himself to reconcile His creation back to glory through grace (Ephesians 2:8-9). How can this be done, you might ask? The scripture says, "Faith comes through hearing the message" (Romans 10:17). The scripture also tells us "Beautiful are the feet of those who bring good news." Now, I don't know how pretty my feet are but I do bring the good news to the scooter world, my brothers. So again, let me say, "You don't know me but I am your brother."

God has chosen to let Himself be seen in many ways throughout time. One of the ways that God has used through the years has been by using unlikely messengers to proclaim His word. Take me, for instance. I was born in North Carolina, raised on a farm with three other kids. Nothing really special about me, except maybe my knack of getting into trouble.

I started chasing girls at the age of seven, smoking cigarettes at twelve, and stole my first motorcycle at about thirteen. I stole my daddy's liquor, fought at school, and got kicked out of school in my senior year. No, there wasn't anything special about me. I finished high school, only because of my dad and the U.S.M.C. recruiter.

With the Vietnam War calling, I left my 1950 Panhead and went in search of the world. The drinking got worse and I added drugging to the mix. I found the world or maybe it found me. I learned to destroy and kill, and Satan just laughed as his hands tightened about my soul.

In 1971, the U.S.M.C. threw me back into civilization, body and spirit broken, with a huge habit and a hate for everyone. The only place I seemed to fit in was with the clubbers. Drinking and drugging was the max . . . and the talent the corps had given me with a gun and a knife was welcomed, too.

I blew my first marriage in nothing flat, using and abusing everyone that was around me. I wasn't sure if it was Satan I heard laughing in my ears or just myself. It wasn't until my second marriage that I began to ask questions. You know, questions like: Why was I going from clubhouse to bars totally wasted out of my mind? Why was it that every time I turned around, people were looking at me with guns and knives in their hands? If this is all there is, why am I still here? You know, just simple questions.

Then, during a sober time while trying to save my second marriage, I began to hear God speaking to me. I knew He had been there all along but I just wasn't listening. It's amazing how deep inside, we really know but won't admit it.

I had gotten real sick and tired of what Satan had been doing to my life so I turned to Jesus with the crumbs I had left. It was amazing, after I had wasted so much and denied Him for so long, that He still loved me. He reached out and my life changed. My life went from a living hell to being on a mountain top. In the Bible the apostle Paul talked about being the worst sinners and in a blinding flash changed it all . . . Now that's good news, Brothers. I felt just like that apostle, the worst of sinners. I had tried it all and somehow I was still miserable. I was stuck on the losing end again and not understanding why. Then it changed. Maybe not in a blinding flash and definitely not something slick enough to make the television scene. But things were changing. I knew right away and felt it deep inside. I was different.

I found myself praying, even when I wasn't in trouble or in need of something. My prayers were more than just, "Oh Lord, won't you give me a new Harley Davidson." I found myself reading the Bible, God's word, and trying to apply it to my life. Guess what? It actually worked!

Now here I am, five years later, with a tent ministry. We travel about 23 states a year, sharing the gospel with the scooter world.

We . . . yeah, I said we. God saved that second marriage. That beautiful teen bride is still with me. God is good.

We aren't fancy and we aren't slick, but then I never trusted that when I was in the world. If you are ever at a scooter show, rally or backwoods throw down and you see a sign that says CHRISTIAN RIDERS MINISTRY, come over and meet your brother . . . you'll be welcome, brother.

For more information write or call:

Christian Riders Ministry, Inc.
P.O. Box 5480
Hudson, FL 34674
Phone: (800) 942-9304 access 206053

# Hell's Angel To Heaven's Saint

## Barry Mayson

The only way out was death! That was the rule of the organization — the Hell's Angels, probably the most feared and notorious motorcycle gang in the country. They were out to get Barry-Barry. He had not been willing to carry out their orders and by their unwritten code, he must die!

The restaurant was surrounded by rough-looking dudes waiting on Barry-Barry to come out. He knew that he might die – the Hell's Angels didn't play around. In fact, the very reason for his being on the West Coast was to attend the funeral of one of the "brother angels" who had been shot in the back three times. This was also to be Barry-Barry's proving time. Although he had lived through the prospecting year — a period of trial association with the Hell's Angels — and although he wore the Hell's Angels jacket, he still had to pass their final test. Barry was given orders to eliminate several members of a rival club back on the East Coast.

The year of a trial, a jacket with Hell's Angels on it, and a lot of rough times, had not completely hardened Barry-Barry. On the surface he was "tough," one to be feared. But inside a raging war was taking place. (Ephesians 6:12: "For our struggle is not against flesh and blood but against the rulers, against the authorities, against the powers of his dark world and against the spiritual forces of evil in heavenly realms.") How many times had he struggled just to keep up with terrorizing activities of the club. What an effect it had taken not to show any sign of weakness. There was a storm raging on the outside, but a veritable war on the inside. How did Barry-Barry get into this mess? What had led him to this place 4,000 miles from home — a point of being filled with fear, knowing that certain death waited just outside the door?

Charles Barry Mayson's early childhood was fairly normal, similar to that of thousands of other boys across the United Stated. He lived in a good home and was taught right from wrong. His childhood activities included attending a Baptist church with his parents. Like many others at the young and tender age of nine, Barry made a profession of faith in Jesus, and was baptized in water. Barry did not, however, experience the reality of Jesus.

Everything sailed along smoothly until I was sixteen, and then my world came apart. My stepfather, who was a real father to me, caught malaria. He was a pilot for Pan American Airlines and was in England when the illness struck. The doctors notified my family that he was in a coma and that his kidneys had ceased to function. The only prognosis for Ben Mayson was death.

It was easy to fall back to earlier experiences. In my need and desperation, I petitioned God for help. I asked God to spare my father's life, but one week later he died! Deep down, I knew that I had no faith, that God had not really heard my prayer. (Psalms 66:18 "If I regard iniquity in my heart, the Lord will not hear me." Isaiah 59: 2 "But your iniquities have separated between you and your God, and your sins have hid his face from you, that He will not hear.") With my father's death, I lashed out at cursing Him, denouncing the whole idea — even to saying that there was no God. (Proverbs 28:14 "Happy is the man that feareth always; but he that hardeneth his heart shall fall into mischief.")

The rest of my time in high school was filled with turmoil. My grades dropped; I started drinking and getting into trouble. I resented authority, especially that of my mother and including that of my teachers as well. I cheated my way through high school, graduating with others who had earned their diplomas.

Somehow I managed to be accepted by a small Baptist college in the mountains of Georgia. I was going there at my mother's insistence — all I had in mind was having a good time. Eventually I was thrown out for bad behavior.

I turned to the Army next, but it turned out to be a bummer because I still had the problem with authority.

"Freedom" — the idea began to take root in my mind, until it became an obsession with me. After leaving the Army, I had moved to Atlanta, Georgia, and I was working at the Ford plant there. All this time, I hit upon a way to ensure my freedom. I bought a motorcycle and learned to ride it, and ended up riding with a small club called the Rising Suns which soon became the main interest in my life. Lacking any restraint at all, my new freedom soon led to parties, fights, crime, and drugs. Eventually the police busted up our club and I fled town to keep from going to jail.

At 26 years of age, I settled in Charleston, South Carolina, working in nightclubs, gambling, and continuing in my sinful ways. Soon I began to ride with another motorcycle club, the Tribulators. With this group, I became known as Barry-Barry and seemed to have all the things I wanted — my own way, freedom, and popularity.

Unknown to me, God was still working. I had renounced Him, but He had not renounced me. It took a series of events for Him to get my attention.

In 1973 I came in contact with Hell's Angels and eventually became a member on the East Coast. Thc activities that followed kept me on guard all the time. There were continuous wars. Everything was well organized and secret, but I knew people were getting killed, not who or why, but that it was happening.

I remember the day of October 27, 1976, very well. The Hell's Angels on the West Coast had given me orders to eliminate several members of a rival club on the East Coast. Although I had been participating in terrorist type activities for a year, needless killing just wasn't my bag and the ones that had given me the orders could sense that . . . I had been followed and finally I went into the restaurant, knowing that it represented temporary safety. I knew that if I walked out the door, certain death waited.

I called home, 4,000 miles away. My wife, Gypsey, was staying at my mother's house. On the phone I told them that I was about to be killed, and then I started repenting for the bad life that I had lived. I told Gypsey that I was sorry for the way I had treated her.

All this time, my mother was on the phone, too, and soon she began to tell me just what I needed to hear at that moment. She said, "Jesus died for your sins 2,000 years ago so that you could have eternal life." (John 3:16 "For God so loved the world, that He gave His only begotten Son that whosoever believeth in Him should not perish, but have everlasting life.")

I thought that I had done too many bad things, that Jesus would have nothing to do with me. I had been on the phone for a long time (the call lasted three hours). In a restaurant 4,000 miles from the only love I knew, I felt fear, loneliness, and emptiness. I stood there on the phone listening to my mother tell me of Jesus' love and forgiveness (Romans 8:32). She also told me of His ability to protect and keep and promised me that He would help me out of the situation, if I would accept Him into my life (John 10:27-30 "My sheep hear my voice and I know them and they shall follow me." 28: "And I give unto them eternal life; and they shall never perish, neither shall any man pluck them out of my hand." 29: "My Father, which gave them me, is greater than all; and no man is able to pluck them out of my Father's hand." 30: "I and my Father are one.")

Hot tears began to stream down my face, right there on the phone. My wife Gypsey had been listening to my mother and she also prayed the sinner's prayer (Roman 10:9 "That if thou shalt confess with thy mouth the Lord Jesus, and believe in thine heart that God hath raised Him from the dead, thou shalt be saved.")

New hope, new joy, and healing power swept over me as Jesus gloriously made me a new creature. I literally felt the arms of Jesus being wrapped around me and holding me. I knew then that I, Barry Mayson, and my wife Fran were born into the kingdom of God (2 Corinthians 5:17 "Therefore if any man be in Christ, he is a new creature; old things are passed away; behold, all things are become new.")

God is faithful and true and He did deliver me from the hand of the enemy that day. And I came to the realization that the Hell's Angels were not my enemy. My enemy was Satan and the powers of darkness. (John 10:10 "The thief [Satan] comes only to steal and kill and destroy; I [Jesus] have come that you may have life and have it to the fullness.") Right now!! Through more miracle circumstances, I was able to escape the death blow of the Hell's Angels and return to South Carolina to my family.

If you would like more information on Barry or the ministry, write to:

Barry Mayson
P.O. Box 8811
Gray, TN 37615

| | | |
|---|---|---|
| There is also a V.H.S. video testimony | | $25.00 |
| | Movie *The Fallen Angel* | $30.00 |
| | Book *Fallen Angel* | $11.00 |

# Harvest Outreach Ministries (Luke 10:2)

## Rev. Allen "Doc" Rogers

I was raised in a Christian home and gave my life to Jesus at a very young age. In my teen years I became both confused and distraught by churches' splits and the differences between the things I read in my Bible and what went on in the churches. I began to fall away and seek fulfillment in other places.

Parties, broken marriages, nomadic wandering and ultimately, involvement in the one percent motorcycle lifestyle followed.

In 1979 I reentered a relationship with Jesus and knew that I was being called into the ministry. I left the "club" and rode 1,200 miles to attend a Bible Seminary. Upon my arrival I was informed that I would not be allowed to attend because of my past.

Within a few years I had returned to an even deeper life as an outlaw, which led to my involvement in an international crime organization.

During 1986 I could tell that God was dealing with me, but it was in 1987 that I removed my moldy Bible from the closet it was hidden in, and opened it.

I was overwhelmed by what God was saying to me as I began to read His Word! I could not believe that I would be allowed to have a relationship with God after all the things I had done. I left the "organization" (not easy!) and promised God that I would for the rest of my life, "seek first the Kingdom of God," (Matthew 6:33), and that my choice for whom I was going to serve (Joshua 24:15) would be Him..

Shortly when I shared the "Good News" with my family they, too, accepted Christ. We did not know how much of a test our faith was soon to be put through.

My wife Pamela had been in poor health for most of her life. She had a bad kidney, requiring weekly treatment of dialysis. Now, we were informed that the doctor had found cancer in her liver, kidney and bladder. The doctor said that she had less than eighteen months to live.

While we were struggling with Pam's health problems added pressure came when we were informed that I would be arrested for many of the crimes I had committed while I was involved with the organization. Also, I struggled with the years I had wasted since my calling to the ministry back in 1979.

I could not comprehend that God could still use me when I had fallen so far. However, one day I was reading in the Word that "both God's call and His gifts are irrevocable" and immediately recommitted myself to the ministry at this time.

I believed that God could heal Pamela. However, if I was going to be running from my past or spending time in prison, it would have been a blessing if her new-found Savior had called her to be with Him.

We moved near my wife's family so that our daughter would have a home if both Pamela and I were absent. An amazing and wonderful thing happened! Upon the doctor's examination of Pamela, no evidence of cancer or kidney problems was found. The doctors were not sure how or why, but she was given a clean bill of health!

The Federal Government had graciously been waiting to sentence me during my wife's illness. Although they never understood how my wife had been healed, they acknowledged the changes I had made in my life and at this time I was allowed to plead to one charge in lieu of the more than forty charges on the indictment.

I spent 1989 through 1992 in Federal prison. I think of it as having studied prison ministry first hand!

I have been living life with Jesus as my #1 priority for nine wonderful years now. I know that to maintain my walk I must spend time in God's word every day and be in regular prayer. Also fellowship with other Christians is very important.

Harvest Outreach Ministries was founded as an inter-denominational non-profit ministry upon my release from prison in 1992.

I am a volunteer chaplain at the local county jail and make regular visits to prisons and county jails in many states. Correspondence with inmates is also a large part of this ministry. We send Bibles and other Christian literature to many prisons across the country. Visits to the families and friends of inmates are made regularly. We try to give follow-up support to inmates when they are released.

Harvest Outreach is also involved with young people and is often called to council troubled youth or to speak at schools. We are sponsors of a local chapter of "Bikers for Christ." We do not limit the realm of this ministry. We seek to be open to the leading of the Holy Spirit in any ministry that we are asked to be a part of.

For more information write or call:

Harvest Outreach Ministries
P.O. Box 211
Bowie, TX 76230
Phone: Church (817) 872-2793
Phone: (817) 872-5170
Rev. Allen "Doc" Rogers

# International Christian Bikers Association

# Pastor Roger Gamble

There Is A Way
An Adventure of Trials, Tribulations
and Victory

My search for peace and fulfillment led me through many rough waters. My way was filled with alcohol, the occult, sex, outlaw Biker gangs and losing large amounts of money. Then one day I realized there was only one way to have true peace. I realized I had spent over 25 years searching in all of the wrong places. I finally know the answer to being fulfilled and having the inner peace I had so longed for.

Where does one begin to tell his story? The struggles, the disappointments, the fears, the loneliness, the frustrations, the anger and even the reason why we were put on this earth?

I suppose one must go back to the earliest times in one's life that he can remember. For some it must go back even farther, yes, even back prior to birth. This is my case, not in any way to justify the way I acted or to use it as an excuse for the way I behaved, for I am responsible for my actions and the choices I have made.

My mother came from a very close knit family, while my father left home at an early age. On one hand we kids could do no wrong and even when we should have been punished it was most often overlooked.

Mom wanted to show love and mercy while Dad, on the other hand, did not know how to share his feelings. As my father was growing up he never heard these simple but powerful words, "I love you."

As a result, Dad and I never knew how to communicate. I always thought he never loved me or at the very least I was not a priority. I felt if I ranked at all it was somewhere well below television or at the very minimum well below everyone else on earth. I had the impression he would go out of the way for strangers but not for me.

I grew up in the age of *Father Knows Best* and other family type shows where fathers and sons could share everything, where love was communicated. My heart yearned for one of those fathers know best talks, a two-way conversation where I could truly share all of my dreams, desires, hurts, and even my fears. As I look back now, I can see how generational traits can affect families in negative ways.

In many ways I had become a problem child with my parents not understanding me or knowing how to handle me. Dad did his best, but since he was not able to communicate his feelings and didn't know how to share in mine, he did what too many fathers do. He spent time working trying to provide the material things, instead of supplying what we kids needed most, the love and affection that only comes with spending time with one's family.

Unfortunately, even my own kids have had to endure my weakness in this area. I know the pain of not knowing how to share my feelings with my children and my wife. I now understand the loneliness that my father had felt all these years.

Although I did not realize it at the time, now as I look back God started trying to get my attention when I was very young. At four or five I remember watching an Oral Roberts tent crusade with him praying for people that waited in long lines to get touched by God. I said to myself, "When I grow up that's what I want to do."

I would like to say that my journey started getting better, but it just worsened. I really wanted to know what life was all about.

As a youngster I got hooked on the old fashioned horror films which helped intensify my desire to know what life meant. This almost uncontrollable desire led me to Ouija boards and the world of the occult.

There were many questions in my life that needed to be answered. Could we communicate with the dead? Was there life after death? What about ghosts? Was there a select but very secret group that could even control others, or maybe give life? Often I would seek to communicate with the departed or experiment with spells, always seeking for the very purpose as to my existence.

My pre-teen years were years of confusion, loneliness, frustration while my teen years brought increased rebellion. There was a major battle raging in my life, part of me truly wanting to do good and help others, while the other part could care less what happened to them. All I wanted to do was to please myself and it did not matter who got hurt or what I had to do to have my desires met.

Deep down inside I knew what I really wanted. I needed someone to say "You can make it, you can be someone, you are loved." Someone to share my dreams and fears and to accept me for who I truly was and not what they thought I was.

We all need to be loved and accepted, whether we admit it or not. This wanting to be accepted led me, as a teenager, to start drinking and eventually to join an outlaw Biker club. It was easy to feel apart for we acknowledged we were different; in fact, we were outcasts.

For myself I really believed that because of all my wrong ways I would never make it to heaven, so why not get worse, for the really bad ones would rule in hell. In the state of mind I was in I decided that I might as well hook up with Satan and rule with him. (I had truly bought into a lie that many fall into.)

Although I do not want to focus on all of the garbage I was into, I did want to mention a few areas, so you that are reading this will know that God's mercy is reaching out to you even now. Friend, though your background might not be the same, Jesus is still reaching out to you at this very moment. The choice is yours whether you accept or reject his love that he has available for you.

Before my acceptance of Jesus as my Lord and Savior my life was filled with alcohol, and living a self-serving lifestyle. It also included a time in jail. In fact, there was very little that I was not involved in. We are all trying to fill that void that is in our life.

God was trying to get my attention in many ways, from the early television programs to a time in my teens when I saw a giant cross hanging in the sky for about seven to ten days.

I even had an unknown pastor send a letter to the parole board recommending that I should be released from jail. Another miracle is that my wife stood by me, though I in no way deserved it. The last year before my conversion I wasted about $100,000.00 on a very selfish lifestyle while forcing my wife to live on $5.00 a week allowance.

My conversion came when a friend pointed out a book by Don Basham called *Deliver Us From Evil.* Probably one of the biggest battles of my life came when I started to read this book. Part of me wanted to read it, while the other wanted no part of it.

On April 27, 1977, I realized that all the ways I had been searching for peace and contentment and even the reason why I should live (that void in my life that I had tried to fill so many ways) could only be filled by accepting Jesus into my life as Lord and Savior.

It would be great to tell you that every area of my life changed at once but I can't. Some did change immediately; others have taken years while some I am still working on. The big difference is that now I have a friend that will never leave me or forsake me. A friend that is very patient, loving and most of all he truly wants the best for me whatever the cost. Jesus gave his life that I might live, not only now but forever.

It has been quite a journey since 1977 and I have learned about the power of the spoken word. You see, for many years both before and after I gave my life to Jesus it always seemed that I would only go so far and then bail out when the going got rough. Sometimes even when victory was in sight I would bail out only to start all over again.

One day God revealed the reason why I was on this merry-go-round. He reminded me of a teacher that had said I would never make it, that I would never amount to anything, that I was a loser.

Friends, you see all my life I wanted to prove to her and others that they were wrong. Unfortunately, after a while the power of those words would take over and I would give up.

For years I feared that when the chips were down and the going got rough that as in my childhood no one would be there for me. For, you see, I had bought into a lie that I would never make it, that

I was a loser. This, combined with my earthly father not being there for me, caused me to fear that God would not really want to help me, either.

Many of us today need to allow God to heal our past, so we might truly see who he is. Far too many believers have a false concept of who God is. We often view him through the eyes of our earthly father or some other authoritarian figure. Why not, right now, ask God to set you free.

Friends, the good news is God will never leave you. He will never forsake you. God truly wants to see us restored. He wants to restore to us the years that we have lost to sin, loneliness, rejection, fears, etc.

We have all made mistakes and as a parent of three boys, I know the pain of not being the parent I would have liked to be. We must not use this as an excuse for not trying. Many Christians carry a great deal of pain, unforgiveness, bitterness, anger, and the hurts they have felt from the way others have spoken to or treated them.

These feelings and emotions should have been given to God many years ago. God knows all about them and he understands the toll it has taken on us. But it's our choice, yours and mine, whether we give it up or continue to allow it to hinder our life. Let us quit using excuses and grow up. We need to come out from behind the masks and walls and let God set us free.

For years I carried a lot of pain for the wrong choices I made in my life. As I allow God access to every part of my being, He is removing all the feelings of hurt, loneliness, anger, and confusion out of my life.

Jesus is leading me into a more fulfilled life as I allow him to mold and shape me in every area. I believe we need to stop living in the past and press forward to the mark of the high calling of God in Christ Jesus (Philippians 3:14).

We need to quit blaming others and stop trying to justify our actions. It is an important step to let God restore us. It is vital for us to understand that God has a vision, a plan for our lives, and as we give him access he will bring it to pass (Psalm 1:1-3).

There have been many times when I have felt like giving up, but why would anyone want to go back to a life of misery and pain? I have found out that during those times I was walking in my own strength.

As we learn to walk in his empowering presence there is victory and life abundantly. The Christian walk is not an easy one, but it is the only one that will end in total victory (1 John 1:7).

I would like to challenge you to give God all of those hurts that you are carrying and give him access to every area of your life. Next time you give him some of those feelings of rejection, abuse, loneliness, doubt, fear, etc., please remember not to pick them up again but leave them at the foot of the cross.

In closing I would like to say to my parents, you did the best you knew how. I do thank you for all you have done. I love you both.

To my children, you are my joy and treasure. I thank God for allowing you to be part of my life. Try to learn from my mistakes and always, always make God number one in your life. Jeffrey, Barett, and Jason, you are special, you can make it as you follow God. You are loved.

To my wife, what words can say what I feel? You have stood with me when others did not. You not only carried all of the pain and abuse of your life, but always found some way to carry mine as well. Thank you for walking those extra miles with me. You truly are one of God's treasures.

The most important is my Lord and Savior Jesus Christ. He has given me the reason for living. He has saved me from myself and given me hope for now and eternity. He loved me even when I did not love myself. God is molding and shaping me so his perfect love can be manifested to a world that so desperately needs to feel his warm embrace.

Most of you know the story of Christ's birth and how there was no room for him at the inn. I pray that you don't let that be the case when he knocks at your heart's door. I truly hope that you will make the right decision, for whatever you decide will be for an eternity.

There is absolutely only one way to have true peace and eternal life. There are many who will say this is the way, or this can be the way. But, Jesus says he is the way and no one comes to the Father except through him.

Why not ask him into your heart today? He is reaching out to you right now. Don't put it off — Jesus is saying come!

Thank you, Jesus, for everything.

In his service,

Roger Gamble

For more information write or call:

I.C.B.A.
c/o Roger Gamble
455 - 21 - 10405 Jasper Ave.
Edmonton, Alberta
Canada T5J 3S2
Phone (403) 459-2461

# Jesus Loves A Scooter Tramp, Too!

This is Tramp's story. Dad and Mom gave me the name "Everett," but my granddad called me "Tramp" and that is what my friends call me. My parents raised me up in the knowledge and fear of God, and faith in Jesus Christ, but I always questioned this faith. The God my dad told me about was so loving and powerful that I could not see anyone messing with His folks. Dad and Mom were very gentle and I mistakenly equated the meekness I saw in them with weakness.

Tiny (my granddad) was an alcoholic and a large, powerful man that no one messed with if they knew what was good for them. I watched and began to see that if people feared you, life seemed to run much smoother. Tiny always had a laugh or a prank that he was pulling on someone. Tiny gave each of his granddads a nickname that he called them all the days of his life, amen. Tiny was not meek and was not weak and I did not want to be weak. I did not see how enslaved Tiny was to the alcohol, or how he regretted the mean things he had trashed — all I saw was Tiny.

There were some Bikers in the neighborhood I grew up in and my mom was friends with one of the wives, a woman named Peggy. Peggy's husband Chic took me on my first motorcycle ride on his big, shiny, blue Harley Davidson Panhead, and I was snakebit from then on with being a Biker! I watched people get out of these Bikers' way and I thought that I had found the way to be happy; but life went on and all that life does, it did to me.

When I was fourteen, I was hit in the head. This caused a cerebral hemorrhage, resulting in a coma, thus ending any thoughts of high school football or any contact sports. This also ended my dream of one day being in the Navy. Contact sports were out but I loved a good fight! The boy who went into the coma and the boy who came out of the coma were two different boys! When I came to, I became aware of an anger that I had never known before, a rage that was consuming, but at the same time, I had absolutely no doubt that God Almighty had touched me and brought me back from the brink of death. I decided that I would take another real close look at this God my parents worshipped. I paid more attention and even read the Bible on my own and I found a major gap in what my father taught me and what I saw the church folk doing. The gap I found in what the Bible said and what I was, was even more astounding, but I did not see that we all have our own personal wars to fight in spiritual realms. These people were not perfect, nor were they really supposed to be — they were forgiven sinners!

At any rate, the call of the Biker lifestyle was calling me. I was drinking in the bars and running with all the little barroom cuties I could and I lost interest in church, God, and anything that would cut my fun short. I became involved with a long-legged girl who at one time had flown a property patch of a club member and while drinking with her in a bar, her ex-old man came in with some bro's and joined us; we kind of stared at each other and sized each other up for what seemed like eternity and I told him that his bro's would surely get me but he would die before me. He laughed and said, "You're cool, let's party," and I began to descend into a nightmare world of drugs, alcohol, violence, sex, hatred, and rage like I never imagined possible. All of my life, what I had longed for was to belong, just belong, and now I belonged to a brotherhood of hatred and violence. The power I felt was more intoxicating than any drug or drink, more seductive than any woman, and more damning than I thought any hell could be. The freedom I imagined was lost in the organization and machine of the club. The fun was soon replaced by club business. The club became an all consuming god who drank the very humanity out me until all that was left was a rabid animal, looking for someone to hurt.

Dad and Mom never quit praying for me, they never locked me out, their home was always open to me, and I knew I was safe there with them. When I had gone too long without food or sleep, all wired out on speed, I always ran home to crash. I never wore my colors to my folks house or carried my guns there. Never did I take my drugs into their home because that was my safe spot.

The Bible says what a man sows he reaps and my harvest came to fruition in July 1973 when a bunch of us were arrested for killing a member of a rival gang. This man died with his head cradled in my hands. I watched him die as the light left his eyes and his soul was taken into eternity. It has been over twenty years and at night in my nightmares I watch that person die over and over again. While in maximum security in Montgomery County Prison, I had a lot of time to think. The drugs wore off and I could think clearly for the first time in a long, long time. I could hear the God of my fathers asking me, "What are you going to do now, stupid?" and because I had grown up with Dad and Mom telling me what needed to be done I knew I needed to ask Jesus Christ to forgive the multitude of my sins and come into my heart and life as Savior and Lord. I knew for the first time in my life that without Jesus, I was absolutely and totally damned with no hope.

In that prison cell, I called upon the name of Jesus and I was born again. By the grace of God, the charges were dropped from me and I have had the chance to live my life for Jesus. It has not been easy. That rage still knocks at the door of my heart, the drugs still call out to me, all the vile things I did haunt me, but I know that Jesus Christ paid for it all on Calvary and I am a child of God washed in the blood of the Lamb!

There have been failures, but the victory I have in Jesus outweighs any failure. I have learned by very bitter experience that the world has nothing to offer but headache. Jesus is all I need to be happy, accepted, fulfilled and acceptable to God the Father.

Now we get to you, and you must decide for yourself what you're going to do with this gift of salvation Jesus Christ is offering to you. Maybe you have not sunk to the levels of sin that I did, but you have your own sins to account for and that is enough to damn you if you reject the grace of Jesus Christ! So it is up to you.

For more information write:

Everett "Tramp" Barger
Heaven's Saint M.C. Ministry
Box 7311
West Trenton, NJ 08628

# R. C. Crusade For Jesus

## Rick "Angel" Kensler

I was born in Huntington, West Virginia, on September 25, 1954. For some reason, my mother Charlotte sent me to live with my Uncle James and Aunt Eunice when I was six months old. They became my mother and father and raised me in Ohio. James was my mother's brother. My real father I never knew. They have told me that his name was Karl Berry. I have three brothers and four sisters with another sister being dead. James and Eunice helped raise an older brother and sister. We were poor but James worked hard to make sure we had a roof over our head and food on the table, the basic necessities but no real luxuries. I was brought up to be my own man and not to run from things. Dad was not easy but at the same time he was not hard. If you got out of line you were asking for a spanking. Although I wasn't brought up in church, James and Eunice did instill a strong sense of morality and ethics into my life. Unfortunately there was no mention of Jesus.

By the age of seven or eight I knew James and Eunice were my aunt and uncle but I called them mom and dad anyway. This kind of made my other brothers and sisters and real mother a bit upset. I felt that just because my mother birthed me didn't mean she was my mom. Eunice was the one who cared for me and raised me. I remember being in grade school fighting. I was taught never to start a fight but to finish one. By the age of ten, I started to think that the older I got the more I was supposed to mature. This was also the time when we moved to town from the country. I began going to city school with a lot of kids who had parents with money. They tended to make fun of me and what I wore so I began fighting. I was promoted from fourth grade to the sixth grade because I was ahead of my class. In sixth grade, I was placed in special education due to my inability to get along with my classmates. This made me even angrier because, to me, this was a retarded class and I believed I could do anything I put my mind to. My attitude became "You want a retard, I'll show you a retard!" I suppose this was when I became really rebellious. In 1967, I remember older kids trying to take my lunch money but I couldn't see it. My dad worked hard for that money. I began to push back and eventually began to take their lunch money or whatever I wanted to take. My friends and I started a street gang called "The Delaware Night Riders" in 1969. That year, I was expelled from school for repeated incidents of fighting. Judge Barit said I was "a menace to society" and he never wanted to see me in school again. All this because I broke the jaw of a rich kid, "Jeff Foster." This was okay with me since I didn't like school anyway. I do wish someone would have told me that the constitution guarantees every citizen the right to an education.

By 1971, at the age of seventeen, I had been to court seventeen times and thrown in jail 21 times. With all this excitement, Judge Barit decided to commit me to the Boys Industrial School in Columbus, Ohio.

I was sentenced to six months to one year for attempted murder. After serving three months, I escaped. I didn't do rules well so my time there was unproductive. The staff and other kids told me that escape was impossible but I considered myself smarter than the average boy. So I proved to them that they couldn't catch me. I returned to Delaware to see my girlfriend. I stayed with my buddy Rudolph for three days with the cops roaring all over the place. After three days I came to Marion where my Uncle Jessie tried to turn me in but once again I outsmarted them. After about a year I called the youth commission and convinced them to send me my release papers since their attempts to rehabilitate me had failed. I told them that I was the only one who could change my life and they agreed.

About this time, at the age of eighteen, I was married. I married not for love, but to prove to the authorities that I had settled down. We were living in Marion. I had a good job driving trucks for Mitchell's Bakery and owned my own dump truck which earned me a good living. All went well until my wife started nagging me and accusing me of going out on her. Finally I did what she had been accusing me of and left her, the job, and the dump truck in that order.

I met another woman and we moved in together. We had two children, Ricky James and Casey Joe, a girl. By the age of 21 I became involved with a motorcycle club, the "Avengers." At the Caboose Bar in Marion on November 28, 1975, at ten p.m. I was shot by a nine millimeter bullet. My son was six months old. The bullet entered above my heart, went through my lungs and exited a hair from my spine. I listened as the doctor told my dad that I had a fifty-fifty chance of dying. After thirteen days in the hospital, I was released with a paralyzed arm and a new sense of vulnerability. My new motto became "You can't kill superman without Kryptonite bullets."

The rage and violence inside me ballooned for the next seven years. My involvement in crime also progressed to include prostitution, drugs, and strong arming for hire. I delighted in the fact that a disabled man could still whip up on the world. I also became involved in demonology and numerology. From eating acid, smoking grass, and drinking there were times when I thought I was the devil himself.

After eight years together, my woman decided she couldn't handle me being gone all the time, the partying, and the Biker scene. She asked me to leave and I obliged her.

In 1974 my mom Eunice became confined to bed. She was ill for eight long years. On December 19, 1982, she died. During her illness, I would stop by and stay with her a few days. I don't remember exactly when but on one of the days I was with her I noticed she was watching TV 39, a Christian station here in Marion. She would lay there praising the Lord and thanking Jesus and asking him to take her home. Well, not being raised in church and not hearing things like this before was a shock. I was convinced that her illness and the medication was making her crazy. Two days before she died, as we were taking her to the hospital again, she told me she was going home. I told her "No, mom! You are going to the hospital. Then you will be coming home." I did not understand. She had begun to tell me that I needed to change my life and turn to Jesus. Of course, I thought she was crazy and paid her no mind.

A couple of years later, I quit drinking, drugging, and hanging with the motorcycle club. While at a Biker party, there were three clubs partying together and as the night wore on and everyone got drunker and higher they began fighting among themselves. I was outside and looking up at the club house and I didn't see brothers anymore. It seemed as if I was watching a pack of demons.

After six months of sobriety, a couple of guys started coming to my motorcycle shop to tell me about Jesus. Every Sunday they were sure to stop in to tell me how much I needed Jesus. They aggravated me by telling me I "needed" Jesus. I didn't "need" anything or anyone. I really wanted to punch their faces.

In March of 1986 at about three a.m. God spoke to me. I wasn't going to jail or dying, I was simply working. God spoke in a small voice telling me that I'd lived wicked all my life and unless I changed my soul would spend an eternity in hell when I died. It was like a mini video playing back all the evil things I'd said and done. I was afraid for the first time in my life. Well, I must have accepted Jesus then, for the rest of the day I couldn't wait to be done.

That evening I called Mike, one of the guys who had witnessed to me at the shop. I hadn't spoken to him in about a year but he knew who I was immediately. He told me that God had just shown him that I wanted to start going to church. That night I went to church and it was the beginning of a whole new life and nothing has been the same since.

I thought I would just sit in church till Jesus came back but it didn't work that way. He began to open a lot of doors for me. I became director of a Bible Rescue mission from 1986 to 1989. During that period, some of my responsibilities included financial planning, public relations, and counseling individuals in the physical, mental, and spiritual areas of their lives. Most of my work involved transients, alcoholics, drug addicts, and the mentally ill. We also provided meals, clothing, and shelter to these people.

God has directed me back to the streets where I came from to minister to the hard core, unwanted class of people. I returned to school to obtain a high school diploma and went on to earn a bachelors degree in psychology in 1989. I never thought I would get through that but God said one day at a time and with help from my guidance counselor this got me through the longest period of my life. Out of fifty psychology books, I only found five to be Christian based. I continued my studies to earn a masters degree in psychology in 1990 and went on to earn a second masters in guidance and counseling in 1993. I say this not to brag but only to point out that this has been accomplished because of God's blessing and directions.

As never before, God has placed in my heart a burning love and compassion to reach people of the street and to those in need. Since my conversion experience in 1985, I have been involved in rescue missions and street and jail ministries. In 1987 I began R. C. Crusade for Jesus, which stands for Radically Concerned, to reach out to the outlaw Bikers, prostitutes, and street people all over the world. Although I am an ordained minister, the Lord has impressed on me the need to continue my education. I also have written a book called, *Street Ministry Guide And Tips*. And if you are reading this book it is my second one. You just don't know what the Lord has for you.

Remember also that "being confident of this, that He who began a good work in you will carry it on to completion until the day of Christ Jesus" (Philippians 1:6).

We also have a Christian Biker magazine called *Full Throttle With Christ*, a Biker Bible, and a street gang Bible.

For more information write or call:

R.C. Crusade For Jesus Ministry
P.O. Box 1423
Marion, OH 43301-1423
Phone (614) 382-3633

# Sons Of God
# Roy "Moggie" Levingston

I grew up in a small town in Ohio, and am the youngest of three children. I bought my first motorcycle working for my dad on the trash route that he owned and operated. My brother and his friends were my inspiration to get interested in motorcycles. They rode dirt bikes and street bikes. Sometimes they would take me along.

At thirteen years old, I got my first motorcycle. I was hooked on riding and began to go racing with my brother. At sixteen years old, I got my car and motorcycle permits the same day. After I got my license, I got my MC endorsement about two weeks later.

I spent most of my time and efforts in my teen years learning what females were all about. Somehow I managed to graduate and get a good job. This resulted in a lot of partying with women and racing dirt bikes, something I really love doing. Doing all of this, and more, was filling my desire at this time of my life. All of the sinning and racing were leaving me broke. Not being able to find a sponsor, I could not go any farther in my racing career, so I decided to get out of it and get a Harley. After buying one of the American dreams, I started to hang around with others who rode Harleys and the things that they were doing seemed to fit right in to my kind of lifestyle.

I was 22 when I got my first Harley, then at 24 something started to happen to me. I was noticing a lot of things on television and around me about Heaven and Hell. I was even sitting in a bar with a friend and the conversation got on the subject of heaven and Hell. By thinking I was not that bad of a guy, I thought, "If I die that night I would make Heaven." But when my friend stuck his finger in my face and said you and me and all these people in this place are going to Hell, it sparked a wakening in me like a sledgehammer hitting me in the face. This really started to bother me. Then some time after that I was having coffee with a friend, and he had just given his life to Christ. He told me all I had to do was to ask Jesus to forgive me.

That night while lying in bed, I asked Jesus to forgive me of my sins, and to come into my heart and be my savior and Lord. That was the beginning of a whole new and different lifestyle. The prodigal son had come home. I started my relationship with Christ by talking to him and reading a simplified Bible, *The Book*. About six months later, the same friend asked me to go to church with him. When I went to church I found that the people there were real, and were not ashamed to share the love of Jesus with me. They accepted me as I was, long hair and jeans.

After being in church a while, I thought Harleys and church did not mix, so I asked the Lord what he wanted me to do with my motorcycle. The Lord said unto me as long as it doesn't come in between you and me, go use it for my glory. A short time after that I met Gary Shire, the founder of the SONS OF GOD, a Christian motorcycle club. I started to hang around with them and go to their Bible study. In December I became a member.

If you are wondering how I got the nickname Moggie, it was when I was eight years old. We went to stock car races. I always rooted for a guy named Moggie, so my dad gave me that nickname, and it stuck.

As I started getting involved in the ministry, I caught the vision to share the gospel and love of Jesus Christ to Bikers of all sorts and anyone else who came in to my path. When God puts a calling on our life he gives you the strength and power to fulfill that calling.

After about a year in the club I became the chapter president. While continuing to pray for vision and direction, the SONS OF GOD M.C. became a solid tool for the Lord, with many trials and tribulations.

The club kept growing with the whole intent to do the great commission as found in Matthew 28:18-19, with chapters in seven states. After being around for ten years, I was voted in as the National President. If I would die today, I would like to see the ministry still going strong all across the nation, being a very fruitful tool for the gospel of Jesus Christ.

God is interested in a relationship with someone just like you, so draw near to him and He will draw near to you.

You can write or call for more information:

SONS OF GOD M.C. MINISTRY
P.O. Box 1169
Lorton, VA 22199
Phone (703) 550-7275

# The Testimony Of A Man Called Hammer

## Charles T. Hughes

Born March 5, 1945, in Penn Argyl, Pennsylvania, I was the first-born of three children of Lloyd L. Hughes and Sarah T. Hughes. My parents were both U.S. Marines. At the time of my birth my dad was in the Philippines, and my mother was sent to my dad's hometown to have the baby. I was loved by all and stayed with my mom at my aunt's house until my dad returned from the war. Soon after his return our little family loaded everything we had in a 1928 Essex car and headed for Gilmer, Texas. I entered the great state of Texas at the age of fourteen months and have remained, for the most part, ever since. My parents were responsible and hard working citizens. My dad was a steel worker and through the G.I. Bill, my mother became a school teacher. My dad is retired and lives nearby; my mom died in 1980.

I was raised to be a patriotic, hard working middle class citizen. I tried very hard to be just that. I was, as a young person, very active in church, 4H, and FFA. I played on the high school football team. I married one of the majorettes after a four year courtship.

At the age of sixteen I became a licensed Baptist preacher. I was doing everything I thought I should; however, I never did seem to be what my ? would have me to be. In 1965 I received my greetings from Uncle Sam. I had been married about eighteen months, Vietnam was cranking up, and the cool thing was to go to Canada. Because of my upbringing and my desire to please, I knew I not only had to go, but I had to be a United States Marine. I entered boot camp in February, 1966, M.C.R.D. San Diego, California. I was too fat, but I had a determination second to none. I graduated from boot camp with the highest score on the rifle range, and a meritorious promotion to the rank of PFC. After two more months of training, I got my orders for Vietnam. After a thirty-day leave I was soon in the country. I was assigned to FLSG - B Trk Co., attached to the 1st Marine Division ChuLai. I did my job well. After five months we were split up because our base was being turned over to the 1st. Air Cac., and we were sent north. I ended up at Red Beach just outside of DaNang. I continued to function as I was directed. I acquired the rank of Corporal E - 4 in just eighteen months of service. I was no longer the little boy from Gilmer. I was as hard as nails. I had seen so much death my blood had turned to ice water.

I remember on one occasion, to prove this point, I took a G.I.'s pet duck from him and bit the duck's head off. I threw the flailing body of the duck at his feet and laughingly handed him the duck's head. I had witnessed an explosion while on convoy on Hwy. 1 that took the life of a friend and all the troops he was hauling; we only found pieces of them. I had also made several trips hauling comrades in body bags, stacked like hay, to their ride home at the air base. I believe the most devastating part of the whole thing was the reports from home. We could believe the hippies were burning flags, but I could not believe they were getting away with it. How could my dad and others sit and let this happen while we were trying so desperately to save it with our very lives? My time in country finally passed. I will never forget that 707 at Kedena AFB pulling up for us to board. I remember thinking, "I've finally arrived! I was a good kid growing up. I've served my country and survived. I have earned the right to be a respected citizen of my country." I would get a good job, build me a nice house, enjoy my wife and family and above all be respected, because I did not run, I had fought the good fight.

The flight was 24 hours long. We slept most of the way. Upon arrival at Eltoro Marine Air Station we got a paycheck and a taxi to L.A. International. It was here I got my first inclination that things might not be as I thought they would be. I was shunned at the airport like I was a killer or something. I was shunned in Dallas Love field by my dad. He was disappointed that my uniform was a mess. You see, it had been in a seabag for a year in storage. They said, “Dig it out and put it on and get on the plane.” My wife was not there because she couldn’t get off work. I had Dad take me to her apartment where I waited for her to come home. When she did I got the Dear John news. I could not believe it. I had her take me to a big shopping center at the edge of Dallas the next morning. I got out of the car and hitched my way home to Gilmer. This is the part they never taught me about; it wasn’t supposed to be this way. I finished my time in the corps, got an honorable discharge, drank a lot of beer and did a lot of thinking and crying. Within three months I met my present wife, Jamie. She had two kids and her husband had deserted her. We married ninety days after we met. I was not fit to be a husband. I could not trust anyone. I did not trust her, my country, or anything else.

I shifted around from one job to another, and drank a lot of beer. I blamed her for our problems because she just didn’t understand. The television news reports seemed to confirm all my suspicions. More than once I would go into great rages and break up furniture and destroy the television. When the guys in Canada were given amnesty, that was the straw. We had a brick home by this time and good cars. I almost gave the house away and bought a patch of woods away from everyone. I built a shack for six hundred dollars and proceeded to get as far from society as I could. I knew the more things I had, the more dependent I would be on the system so I did without and tried to live off the land. I would go to Louisiana to buy fish and bring them back and peddle them. I also grew and peddled veggies. I raised and butchered my own hogs. I even bootlegged a little white whisky. Mom died in 1980 very disappointed in her #1 son. My inheritance from her death allowed me to open a fish market which soon became a Cajun restaurant. It was successful until the oil field crunch in 1982; in ’83 it became a saloon and a year later I was broke again. Somewhere in this time the governor started paying for abortions. I quit paying taxes at that point and tried to be invisible.

The few months I had the bar proved to be a great turning point in my life. I had decided to get a divorce; I knew there was no hope for our marriage. Jamie had asked me if I would go to a marriage counselor. I had no use for folk like that but I went so I could say I had touched all the bases. In our conversation it was mentioned that I was a Nam vet. The counselor mentioned that there was a vet group in Longview that had a baseball team and that I might be interested in going to a game. I thanked him but I was not even remotely interested. After the session, Jamie and I both agreed that it was wasted time. This ball game that had been mentioned was two weeks away. It came to my mind about three days before time, and I couldn't shake it. The afternoon before the game was to be at seven I knew I had to go, although I didn't know why. I called Jamie and explained what I had been experiencing and asked her if she would come in that night and run the bar. I got to the ballpark early and just set in the car. After a while a car showed up. The guy got out and I noticed his jersey. It was black and it had a map of Nam on the front in white. I began to cry uncontrollably. I stayed in the car so I wouldn't be seen.

It was several minutes before I got control of myself. After I did I made my way to this guy. He still was not aware of me. When I tried to speak to him I fell to pieces again and I scared him. I turned and ran into the woods where I hid for over an hour. I watched as the others came to the park and started to warm up. I knew that the guy had reported what had happened because I saw him point toward the woods while he was talking to one of his team mates. I was experiencing a drawing to these guys, like the pull of a great magnet, yet I couldn't get enough composure to go down to them. I picked out their leader and I knew he was a Marine. I gradually worked my way closer and closer; when I exposed myself I was right on top of them. The leader turned to me and stuck out his hand and said, "Welcome home, brother." We both cried and hugged for a long time.

That was in 1983 and I cry every time I remember it. I felt for the first time I really was home. After all those years I had found someone who really did understand what I had been going through. I don't even know who won the ball game, but I know I never enjoyed one more. Their leader was retired Gunnery Sergeant Danny Whyte.

He gave me a brochure that night. I didn't look at it for two weeks. I came in for a nap one day and saw it lying on the dresser.

The title was "Post Traumatic Stress Disorder." I had never heard of such a thing, but when I read the pamphlet I was not only convinced of its validity, I knew I was a victim. I called Jamie and told her about it. I told her also that it had made me realize that this was the cause of our problems and not her as I thought. I told her I would go seek help and we would decide on this marriage problem later. I was assigned to a group therapy program which lasted six months. I went through it twice.

This time in my life did turn things around for me and my marriage was saved. The tragic thing about such programs is that they made me aware of the problem but gave me no cure. I thank God that I went through it. It made me aware so when I got into a certain mind set, or started to react to a situation, I would catch myself and realize why I was acting the way I was. The last time Jamie called my counselor for advice she was told that nothing could be done short of locking me up. It had been over three years since I had gone to bed without at least a half case of beer, wouldn't work without several shots of whisky. If I didn't drink, I couldn't sleep, I only had nightmares and would wake up screaming, totally paranoid.

Somewhere around 1986 I began to experience another magnet drawing. This time it was Jesus. I would send my wife to church but I wouldn't go myself. I had asked Jesus to save me when I was nine years old. I knew I was going to be all right in the great by and by. I sure was not too good in the meantime.

After a fuss, while on a classic drunk, I poured out all my beer and whisky and announced that I was going to church the next time the doors opened. I had been reading my Bible on the sly and had come to one solid conclusion: God Could Not Lie. You see, this had been my big deal, everything I had been taught growing up had not panned out. Patriotism was not the reason we fought wars; it was money. I knew from first-hand experience enough hypocrisy in the church for three men. I talked with Jamie and told her that I was going back to church but with both eyes open this time. If Jesus said it, I would abide by it. But if it was man's doctrine, I would spit it out. At this point in my life Jesus became my redeemer. I could sleep at night, no alcohol, no more dreams.

After about three years of this, with an almost perfect attendance record, I was asked to leave this church because of the way I was believing what I was reading in my Bible. True to what I had promised to do, I left without a fuss to find where Jesus wanted me. I have been in a small nondenominational church for the last four years.

The last three years of my life have been marked with one miracle after another. It all started when Jamie and I asked God to show how we could help others. Remember, we were flat broke and living in a six hundred dollar house. Within two weeks we ran into a person who was stranded where his car had blown an engine. He was from up north somewhere and had his wife with him and had to leave a baby with kin in south Texas. I gave him my pickup and some food, clothes, and a Bible. Within two weeks a man drove up into my yard in a custom Ford van, bucket seats, blinds, the works. He gave me this van. Five days later we felt the Lord wanted us to give it away. This was hard but I told Jamie that I knew God didn't play silly games. If our feelings were correct someone would show up with a need greater than ours. That person was within a half mile of our house. We weren't aware of it until we started looking. The husband had been hurt on the job. He had five kids, no vehicle, and had to travel fifty miles daily to the doctor. I presented him the van title. One month later another fellow approached me and asked if I had been praying for a van. He knew nothing of the first one. I asked him why he asked and he told me God had instructed him to get this van in good mechanical shape so he could give it to someone who needed it.

He was a mechanic. He said he had finished the work and was asking God where to put it and my name kept coming up. I then told him about the first van and he understood. It served me well. About six months later here comes another fellow. God had told him to get me a house. He presented me with a 16X80 mobile home. He bought it, paid to have it moved onto my property, and paid for a $3,500.00 septic system because all we had at the shack was an outhouse.

During this time I was asked to go to Eagle Mountain Motorcycle rally. I rode up with this friend in his car. I slept on the ground in a borrowed sleeping bag without a tent. I enjoyed myself and came home believing God for a Motorcycle. Five months later I had the one that I really wanted at the time, a 750 Honda. Guess what? Two months later, you're right, I gave it away. The man was young and single; it was just what he needed. One week before the next Eagle Mountain I had a 1300 Venture a big step up from the 750. At this rally I really looked hard at the work the C.M.A. was doing, but I really didn't think it was for me. I had a lost friend I had been praying for and I thought maybe if I could get him to go to the changing of colors, he might get saved. Two weeks later he invited me. I was blown away.

When the day came to leave, my scooter was down. He went without me, and God accomplished his work without me. You know he can do that no matter how important we think we are. He came back totally excited. He and some others who went wanted to start a C.M.A. chapter. I went to the organizational meeting just to be polite. After hearing Curtis Clemmonts explain how this C.M.A. worked and their purpose, I realized this was where God wanted me for now. I joined this new chapter and began going to secular rallies to share the word and my Lord. After a short time, I realized my place was with the outlaws. Most of them were vets just like me, but they rode Harleys and hated anything Jap. I started praying for a Harley. One week before the Eagle Mountain Rally guess what! A 1990 Electroglide. I have continued to ride this Harley in his service. In November of this year I was introduced to Bill Glass of Prison Ministries in Beaumont, Texas. April marked the beginning of my full time service as a motorcycle evangelist. Since I got the Harley in mid-September, I have ridden over 30,000 miles. I have made ten weekends in five states, and I have attended numerous rallies while also doing work in local jails. The Lord blessed me with a pop-up camper in July '95. By the end of '96 I will have been in every state in the nation, Canada and Mexico.

For more information write:

Hammer
Rt. 4  Box 618
Gilmer, TX  75644

# To God Be The Glory

## How To Find Your Way With A Wayward Child

He had earned a high position in our local Hell's Angels Motorcycle club by being the toughest abuser of alcohol, drugs, and the law. He was reckless, violent, and pagan. He was my son, Barry.

It's a familiar story. A child who's been nurtured, educated, and loved starts making bad decisions. In Barry's case, the slide started at the age of sixteen when our lives were torn apart by the sudden death of his pilot-stepfather overseas. I'd been so numb with grief that I hadn't worked hard at coping with Barry's rebelliousness. "He'll outgrow this phase," I assured myself. How wrong I was!

Finally the time came when the advice of well-meaning friends pushed me toward rejecting Barry. "Mary, think of yourself, your younger kids. Barry's broken too many promises. Don't let him see you until he straightens up!" These words weighed on my mind on a day I was expecting Barry to stop by. Agonizing over the situation I began to pray, "Lord, help me to know what to do."

Later, when I heard the roar of Barry's motorcycle, I steeled myself for the confrontation, waiting for his impatient rap at the door. Instead, his face popped up at the window, like the playful boy he once was, trying to surprise me. I stared at his long, matted hair, raw, wind droughtened face, tangled beard, his blue eyes. They were my blue eyes, too.

His eyes, my eyes. "Mary," God seemed to be whispering in my ear, "I've never turned you away. Don't turn your son away. It's love that draws people to me." Slowly, I opened the door. "Come in, son," I said evenly.

Some of the hardest years were ahead — Barry even spent some brief stints in jail. Many times I was despondent. With God's help, I found these ways to cope:

1) Let Go, But Keep Loving. You can't control a grown child's behavior, but you may affect him with a loving example. In my case, I hated the way Barry was living, but I was able to show that I cared about him by offering a Saturday afternoon to stretch out in front of my television, a hot shower, a prayer over a home-cooked meal.

2) Show Faith And Grow Faith. Let your belief in God be apparent. One day Barry handed me a bumper sticker that read, "Support your local Hell's Angels." I handed it back. "Son, I can only support the Kingdom of God." Barry looked at me as if I were a humorless simpleton. But later it became evident that, deep inside, he respected my faith.

Through this emotionally trying time, I discovered the comfort of a small prayer group of women with similar concerns. One of them had an alcoholic son, another an estranged daughter. These women helped expand my use of the Bible. In the beginning I didn't know how to pray, and they showed me how to use scriptures as my pattern. I'd find a verse about lost children and ink in Barry's name. Often, I noticed, a prophet likened God's ache for the loss of Israel to that of a parent for a wayward child.

3) Find A Positive Image In The Bible. One night, as I was reading a Bible passage about Moses, I tried to picture the long-haired bearded figure leading a haggard band through the wilderness. Suddenly Barry came to mind, beard straggling to mid-chest, hair flowing over his shoulders. Moses. He killed a man and ran away. But God USED HIM! From that day forward I kept that image in mind when I prayed. God could not only save Barry, but He might also use him!

And, as it turned out, He did both. My prayers for Barry were answered after seven years. My son turned to God — and he also started working in a prison and youth ministry. Other parents may have to wait even longer than I did for a wayward child to come home in spirit. But it need not be time spent alone or in vain. God will gladly share your burdens — and help you grow in love, faith, emotional strength.

Mary Carder (Barry's Mom)

# A Wife, A Partner, A Friend
# DQ Wife Beth's Testimony

I sat in the backyard alone. The backyard was in the town I had been born in, but somehow nothing was familiar. As I pulled the silver flask out my pocket and took a long slow drink, I thought back over the last three days. I had messed up badly. I sure should have seen it coming but the fog had been too thick. Now I was alone, thousands of miles from home and so very much alone. I thumped on the pack of smokes and a joint fell out. I figured I might as well get a buzz from the smoke in my lungs.

As I leaned back my head to fire it up, a star shot across the black night sky. My mind involuntarily repeated the childhood rhyme: "Star bright, star light, first star I see tonight. I wish I may I wish I might, have the wish I wish tonight." I had to laugh at my own foolishness. I learned a long time ago how useless wishing was. Besides, it would take a lot more than a wish to straighten out my screwed up life. In one night, I had lost my husband and my grandma. My old man, well, that was my fault. He could no longer trust me. I broke the bond by a stupid mistake, too many pills and too much booze. It wasn't so much what he thought I'd done. Somehow, it was one in the same. I had lost the only thing in my life that mattered, my first love. My grandma had croaked. I hadn't got to see her before she died. It hurt badly.

As I fired up the joint, another childhood thought crossed my mind. I once knew someone who could make wishes come true. I reached deeply into my fogged brain to find something I once knew. "For God so loved Beth that he gave his only son so that Beth wouldn't die but so that Beth would live forever with Him." I scoffed and cursed out loud, "But I am dying, God. How is that for you? The only man I ever loved and I lost him. Without him, I don't dare to live." I heard a voice say, "Beth, you aren't dead yet." I looked around to see who had said it. No one was there. I sat along in the night, talking to myself. I sat in shock for what seemed an eternity. I looked back up to the sky wondering if it could be true. So many years ago, I had met someone names Jesus. My parents introduced me to Him, but I grew out of it. There had not been time to think about God as a runaway living on the streets. Now, so many years later, could He still be there? I knew then that I had only one shot left. All my other options were gone. Not even realizing the full impact of it, I heard myself say out loud, "God, I don't know if you even hear me but I'll make you a deal. If you give me back DQ, I promise to try to find you. I'll do the church thing and try to read the Bible. I will try God but I gotta have my husband back."

The joint had gone out. The flask laid at my boot. I did not want either at the moment. I put them away and walked into the dark house. The time and space that separated me from my husband didn't matter. Somehow I knew it wasn't over. I knew then, that it was a beginning. Of what, I hadn't a clue, but something was up. I went upstairs and opened a Bible. The years melted away and with them, the pain I had endured. It still hurt, but I knew I no longer had to face it alone.

Within a week, the funeral was over and I flew back to Florida. No one waited for me at the airport. I called DQ and he blew me off saying it was over. I refused to accept that and went home. We fought, cussed, and finally cried. He agreed to try to work it out. God had bought into my challenge. I knew it could only be the Creator of the universe that could change my man's hard heart. It was a beginning. It was the beginning of many things.

God salvaged the marriage and I kept my end of the deal. I started playing church. All I knew how to do was attend on Sunday and act like everyone else. Once in a while, DQ would go with me but the church folks didn't care much for his hair and leathers so I would have to find another church.

But one day, we walked into a real church, full of God's people. They did not see our hair, jewelry, tattoos, and leathers. They saw people who needed the Lord Jesus Christ in their lives. They loved us. The next Sunday, we both gave our lives to Christ and I was baptized into His name. It was four years almost to the day that I had bargained with God. Our lives have never been the same.

It is now 1995. We have been Christians for five years and ordained missionaries for four years. God took two broken people who had wasted everything about their lives and chose to speak to others through them — other Bikers who, just like them, have only crumbs of bread of life left. But God is a God of second chances. He is a God of renewed marriages, cured addictions, and new lives. He is a God of dreams and wishes. And Glory to Jesus, He is a God who loves us enough to have sent his only son to save Bikers, too!

For more information write:

Christian Riders Ministry, Inc.
Attn: Beth
P.O. Box 5480
Hudson, FL 34674

# Born Again – American Outlaw
# "Spanky" Steve Aune

When I saw that drunk Biker on his 1200cc Street Hog climbing straight up that mountain screaming at the top of his lungs, I knew right then, I was entering a dimension of life I had never seen before. (I was sixteen.) Dirt was flyin' everywhere and all his brothers were cheering him on. He was maybe twenty feet from the top when his scooter reared up and rolled over on him. It crushed his leg, mangled it. I can remember him just lying there with a dazed look on his face, and he cried, "Hey, man, I almost made it over the hill." What I saw that day excited me. And then, when my buddy asked me to "Prospect" under him, I backed up, 'cause I knew there was no turning back once you were in. I remember thinking to myself, "Man, these guys are crazy!" It was in my blood.

I remember as a kid the first time I saw a cop hand-cuff a guy, and I can remember the first time I saw a guy get hurt, really bad, in a street fight. My reaction to all this was, "Never get caught and get the other guy before he gets me," whatever the circumstances. I can remember watching people (some friends) losing their minds or dying because they got a hold of "bad drugs."

Well, as you might guess, I figured that kind of mistakes couldn't happen to me. But as smart and cool as I thought I was, I've had hand-cuffs put on me and been thrown in jail. I've been beat up by cops and street enemies, and the drugs I took sometimes weren't always what I thought they were. Speed had me watching a town burn to the ground when there was no town, and the strychnine took me on a trip to "see the devil."

Drinking a quart of Jack Daniels a day meant I could relax and not have to worry just party, party, party! Back when a real party for me was ridin' into a town, takin' what we wanted, then slidin' out to sleep it off. Only to find cops at the door the next day with hand-cuffs and a ride back to that town we trashed.

Probably for me, the worst part of "Outlaw'n" was always havin' to watch my back. I'd screwed and messed with people till I'd never know who's out lookin' for me.

As a kid I grew up in a middle class family, with parents who loved me. We went to church every Sunday and brother, I knew right from wrong. That made life tough, tryin' to fight off a conscience and lookin' for my heart to be hard, "that warfare."

And lookin' in the mirror trying to convince myself. I'm proud but knowin' the scooter I was ridin' was hot, and the Martin D-35 I was playin' was hot, like just about everything else I had. Man, I got mad when some ole boy stole my stolen D-35 guitar. The guy took it while I was passed out with a gun clutched in my hand. I was a partner in the last and final days of this ole rough and tumble bar. It was always packed and there was always plenty of trouble, either from the cops or our loyal customers. Well, somebody had been breakin' in while we were closed and stealin' the money out of the pinball machines. I thought if I spent the night in the club I could catch this guy. Well, sure enough, he came again that night, but things didn't work out the way I planned. I had been drinkin' and was tired and after a while I passed out. While I was sleepin' he broke in and robbed the machines and stole my guitar which was sitting right next to me. I'm lucky he didn't shoot me with my own gun.

I'm not proud of my past, but looking back I can see I was fortunate. I'm alive today and I never served a day of hard time. (Some of my old pals are dead.) Today, I can look my old enemies in the eye and say, I'm sorry and tell them I love them. I can tell them that guy they used to know is dead and buried. I have God in my life now and I've accepted Jesus Christ as my Lord and Savior.

If my story sounds familiar to you or you are a young person who's already taken a few wrong turns in your life, "listen up." God has a better plan for you. If I could do it all over I'd take God's plan for my life over the way my plan turned out. I was pretty smart, and I'm sure you are too, but we're not smart enough. Without God you and I are gonna lose in the end, but with God we can have it all.

One day I found out how much God loved me. He knew I didn't like Christians coming up to me on the streets telling me I was going to hell. He also knew I wasn't ready to give up my women, booze, and drugs. When I had a club I was a fence for some locals, and I remember getting high every time they pulled up at our back door. You could get anything, from motorcycles and stereos to clothes brought in from New York and overseas. And, of course, guns! But God had a plan for me. I didn't know it then, but my chance to find God was coming at me.

My best friend was going straight and I didn't know what he was up to. I hadn't seen him much lately; I just figured it was a woman and left him alone. I didn't have time to worry about him anyway because I was busy keepin' my life jammin'.

Then one day he came around and asked me to come to a get-together at another friend's place. I didn't want to go because I had things to do, but I said okay. I needed to know he was okay. We walked into the apartment and there sat five of my old friends at a table. It was great to see everybody. I noticed not guns, but Bibles, on the table. Man, I can't describe the feeling that came over me when I realized my friends were packin' Bibles. I didn't say a word, I just listened. They started telling me about Jesus and this strange feeling came over me, like something was gettin' ready to happen. I now knew why I hadn't seen them lately. And, man, these are the same people I used to get drunk with, do drugs with, party with, call on Satan with in this ole condemned house we used to live in. And, man, believe me, the Devil lived with us in that ole house. Demons flew in and out of there like it was "Hell on Earth's" bus station. And here these ole friends are telling me about Jesus! But something touched me deep inside that day. When they asked me to go to church with them on Sunday I don't know why, but I said okay. They said the church they went to was called Evangel Temple located just outside of Nashville and their pastor was Jimmy Snow. A lot of Nashville music people went to that church; most of them I couldn't believe at the time could be Christians. Johnny Cash, for example, I was singing his ole drinkin' and prison songs.

When I walked through the door of that church I knew something was gettin' ready to happen. I didn't know if I should stay or run. I felt the power of God pulling me. I didn't know what it was then, I just knew it felt good. Scary but good. When I sat down the power of God came down on me like a freight train comin' down the tracks. Right then I knew there was a real live God and he loved me. When the pastor gave the message I understood what was happening to me and what I was getting ready to do. And when the altar call was given I almost ran down to the front, crying like a newborn baby. As I left church that night I was a newborn baby in Christ Jesus. My life started changing immediately. I set up a meeting with my pastor and asked him what I should do with this "Hot Scooter" I was ridin'. Once he advised me, I knew how to continue with the other things in my life I wanted gone. It felt like I had just lost 100 pounds and I could fly. Twenty years later I'm still flyin', just operate the controls better.

I've shared all this with you for one reason, God has asked me to tell you, he loves you, too. He's asked me to prepare you, just like my friends prepared me. Jesus Christ, God's only begotten son, died for you and me. He shed his blood for us, out of love. I hope I haven't turned you off, because a bad presentation of Christ kept me away for all those years.

I love you, brother/sister, and now is your time to let God and his son Jesus come into your life. It doesn't matter where we are right now, at a bike rally, in a prison or wherever; now is the time to turn to Jesus.

For more information write:

Born Again Biker Ministry
c/o "Spanky" Steve Aune
P.O. Box 84
Sacul, TX 75788

BONDSLAVES Motorcycle Ministry

BOND-SLAVES MC JESUS IS LORD

Gailen 'Mac' Stone
Pres./Chaplain

908 North 7th Avenue
Princeton, Mn 55371
phone (612) 389-4753

---

CHRISTIAN RIDERS MINISTRY

DQ & BETH ROBERTS
Missionaries

P.O. Box 5480
Hudson, FL 34674
800-942-9304 Access 20605

---

*Serving God By Helping Those of His in Need*

Armored
Righteous
Motorcycle
Clubs

Ephesians 6:10-18

(912) 452-7449 (912) 453-9757

---

Servants for Christ — Set Free

First Corinthians 4:1

Set Free Ministry

P.O. Box 722
Dayton, Ohio 45402

Ohio

---

CHOSEN WARRIORS OF GOD

IF WE MEET AND YOU FORGET ME,
YOU HAVE LOST NOTHING:
BUT, IF YOU MEET
JESUS CHRIST
AND FORGET HIM,
YOU HAVE LOST EVERYTHING

ANTHONY, PRES.
813-888-7454

---

JESUS IS LORD — I.C.B.A. — REMNANT

INTERNATIONAL CHRISTIAN BIKERS ASSOCIATION

International President
Pastor Roger T. Gamble

Phone & Fax (403) 459-2461

455 - 21 - 10405 Jasper Ave.
Edmonton, Alberta
Canada T5J 3S2

---

BIKERS FOR CHRIST — BOWIE

If We Meet,
And You Forget Me
You've Lost
Nothing.

If You Meet
Jesus,
And Forget Him,
You've Lost
Everything!

Member DOC (President)
P.O. Box 211, Bowie, TX 76230 (817) 872-1552

---

TRIBE OF JUDAH MOTORCYCLE MINISTRIES

TRIBE OF JUDAH — JESUS IS LORD

Ben & Tammy Priest
(713) 358-7770

P.O. Box 2423
Humble, Texas 77347

FULL THROTTLE
FULL THROTTLE
With Christ Magazine
A MINISTRY OF R.C. CRUSADE
ANGEL KENSLER & BUD BURKE, EDITORS
RALPH STOCK, PHOTOGRAPHER/REPORTER
614-382-3633
P.O. BOX 1423, MARION, OH 43301-1423
REDEEMED
JESUS IS LORD
You Have Just Met...
BIG D
A Servant of Christ Jesus
REDEEMED
MOTORCYCLE MINISTRIES
P.O. Box 748
Brick, N.J. 08723
Phone: 908-255-1580
EPHESIANS 1:7
In Him we have redemption through His blood, the forgiveness of sins according to the riches of His grace.
IF JESUS MAKES YOU MAD
THEN HELL IS REALLY GOING TO
BURN YOU UP!
IT'S YOUR CHOICE
RC Crusade, Inc.
Angel's Street Ministry
P.O. Box 1423
Marion, Ohio 43302
(614) 382-3633
P.O. Box 702
Lima, Ohio 45802
(419) 224-2700
Available for speaking engagements
"He Rides With Me"
Who Rides With You?
WHEELS FOR JESUS
CHRISTIAN BIKERS
"Jesus is Lord"
ALLEN & LIL MOORHEAD
SONS OF GOD
MC
NEW
JERUSALEM
SONS OF GOD MC
P.O. Box 1169
Lorton, VA 22199
or call
703-550-7275
"For as many as are led by the Spirit of God, they are the sons of God." - Roman 8.14
CHRISTIAN MOTORCYCLISTS ASSOCIATION
Ken L. Taylor
MINISTRY TEAM
MEMBER
Mechanical Ministry Team
9660-113 AVENUE • GRAND PRAIRIE, ALBERTA, CANADA
T8V 1W5 • (403)539-4674
CHRISTIAN MOTORCYCLISTS ASSOCIATION
Denise M. Poage
MINISTRY TEAM
MEMBER
Women's Ministry Team
3035 W. TEMPERANCE ROAD
TEMPERANCE, MICHIGAN 48182 313/847-1330
Hardcore International
Ministries
Nelson Campbell
Minister/Mid Atlantic Region
RR2 Box 34
Stanley, Virginia 22851
(703) 778-4543
Central Regional Office:
P.O. Box 261
St. James, Missouri 65559
(314) 265-5951

Servants for Christ
Set Free

First Corinthians 4:1

Set Free Ministry

P.O. Box 711
Anaheim, CA 92815-0711

So. Cal

---

KINGS KIDS
JESUS CHRIST
LORD GOD

IF YOU THROW AWAY THIS CARD
YOU'VE LOST NOTHING
IF YOU THROW AWAY CHRIST
YOU'VE LOST EVERYTHING

Jimmy DiVincenzo
P.O. Box 104
Richfield, OH 44286
TEL.#

---

Christian Motorcyclist Association
Kentucky Chapter, El-Shaddai Chameleons

Dan McFarland
"Biker For Jesus"

P.O. Box 191
Lancaster, Kentucky, 40444

Phone:(606)792-6897
Fax: (606)792-6897

---

**Barry Mayson**
**Prison Prevention Outreach**

P.O. Box 8811
Gray, Tennessee 37615

(615) 477-0317

Eph. 6: 10-21

---

You have been assisted by Rev Mike
one of the 784-8520

Lords Disciples M.C.
1901 E. Minnesota St.
Indpolis, IN 46203

---

RIDING FOR THE SON
HEAVEN'S SAINTS

HEAVEN'S SAINTS CHAPTER
OF THE
CHRISTIAN
MOTORCYCLISTS
ASSOCIATION

P.O. BOX 1467
RIDGEWOOD, NJ 07451-1467

---

**CHRISTIAN MOTORCYCLISTS ASSOCIATION**

***Herbie Shreve***
PRESIDENT

P.O. BOX 9 • HATFIELD, ARKANSAS 71945
501/389-6196

---

**Born Again Biker Ministry**
*Ministering God's Love To All People*

EVANGELIST
BORN AGAIN BIKER
Jesus Christ

EVANGELIST
"Spanky" Steve Aune

member since '91

PO Box 84 Sacul, Texas 75788

HOPE CAFE

CHRISTIAN COFFEEHOUSE

*Where JESUS is our HOPE*

335 E. South St.
Akron, Ohio 44311
216/253-HOPE

HOPE MINISTRY
Drug & Alcohol Support Group
Rev. Lee Miller

---

**JESUS SAVES**

*Righteous Riders*
P.O. Box 1712
Akron, Ohio 44309

BEN CULLY, PRES.
216-699-5538

---

*Behold, I will send my messenger, and he shall prepare the way before me.*
Malachi 3:1

**WEAV**
P.O. Box 31522
Omaha, Ne
68131-0522

---

RUGGED CROSS MC NEW JERUSALEM

You Just Met . . .
BUTCH DE ZUZIO
SECRETARY & TREASURER
48 BUSH AVE
W. PATERSON, N.J.
07424
201-881-8838

Take Up The Cross And Follow Him. *Luke 9:23*

---

*Pastor:* Mark Huffines • (903) 734-5169

***Church of Power***

MOTORCYCLE OUTREACH MINISTRY
Rt. 3 Box 632 • Gilmer, Texas 75644
Col. 1:15-18

*HAMMER "TOM HUGHES" - EVANGELIST*
(903) 725-5560

---

Christ's Disciples
Outreach Ministries
P.O. Box 808

CHRIST'S DISCIPLES
RICHARD (FROSTY) FROST
P.O. BOX 2945
LEESBURG VA 22075
703 430-9245

MOTORCYCLE TEAM

---

**Brother Bert Aguilar****
National President
Soldiers for Jesus M.C.
Servant - Sinner - Saint
Preacher of the Gospel of Jesus Christ
Vato Loco for our Lord - Crazy for Christ
"A Rat, Sharing Where the True Cheese Is"
Weddings Performed, From Jails to Jerusalem
"Keep Oil in your Bike so it won't Burn
Ask Jesus in Your Heart, So You Won't Burn.
Ride Forever with Jesus, He'll Never Leave You."
"Satan Sucks"
The First Person in Paradise was an Outlaw
Write Me. ** "AKA The Gangster of Love"
**Mother Club House:**
(714) 491-8030 • 107 W. Elm • P.O. Box 7 • Anaheim, CA 92815-0007
(209) 578-5012 • P.O. Box 577721 • Modesto, CA 95356

JESUS
JESUS DAVID'S SON
CHRIST

---

Rom. 3:23 Rom. 6:23 Rom. 5:8,10

MOTORCYCLISTS FOR JESUS

Telling
Everyone
About
Messiah

Kari Wardlaw
Road Representative
533-3818
(503)

Acts 3:19 Eph. 2:8 Rom. 10:9-13

IMMANUEL
AMEN
M. M.
Courtesy of
Immanuel
Motorcycle Ministry
White Co.
Member Ruben Lemon (Press)
Phone 501-724-0781
TEXAS
UNDERGROUND
CHRISTIAN BIKER
MAG & MINISTRY
God's Our Master
Jesus Is The Answer
Holy Messenger
Riding For Jesus
Texas Ministry
HOLY MESSENGER -M.M
P.O. BOX 127
CANYON, TX
79015 - U.S.A.
PRAYER-WARRIOR
OUT-REACH #
1-806-655-2548
JESUS
CHRIST
Road Dog
(412) 793-3077
GOD LOVES BIKERS TOO!
LAZARUS GENERATORS
AGE OF GRACE
JOHN 3:16 For God so loved the world that he gave his one and only son, that who ever believes in him shall not perish but have eternal life.
EPH. 1:7 In him we have redemption through his blood, the forgiveness of sins, in accordance with the riches of God's grace.
K.C.
P.O. Box 1574
Jamestown, CA 95327
"A MOTORCYCLE"
"MINISTRY OF"
Set Free Church
1330 W. 3rd St.
Owensboro, KY 42301
(502) 684-3554
SOLDIERS
M
M
FOR
CHRIST
UN-CHAINED
GANG
M
M
Servants of
JESUS CHRIST
Chico
5259 N. Lakeview Rd
Bloomington, IN 47404
(812) 876-9976